GW00362314

The Heavenly Road

John Wesley's journeys in Norfolk and Suffolk

by

Norma Virgoe

The Larks Press

Published by the Larks Press
Ordnance Farmhouse
Guist Bottom, Dereham, Norfolk, NR20 5PF
Tel. 01328 829207

E-mail: Larks.Press@btinternet.com
www.booksatlarkspress.co.uk

British Library Cataloguing-in-Publication Data
A catalogue record for this book is available
from the British Library

**No part of this book may be reproduced in any way
without permission from the publisher and author.**

ISBN 978 1 904006 58 9

© **Norma Virgoe 2011**

THE HEAVENLY ROAD

CONTENTS

ILLUSTRATIONS

'Awake our souls, away, our fears;
Let every trembling thought be gone;
Awake, and run the heavenly race,
And put a cheerful courage on.

True, 'tis a strait and thorny road.
And mortal spirits tire and faint;
But they forget the mighty God
Who feeds the strength of every saint …

Swift as the eagle cuts the air,
We'll mount aloft to thine abode:
On wings of love our souls shall fly,
Nor tire along the heavenly road.

Isaac Watts 1674-1748

Preface

John Wesley travelled extensively throughout his ministry. Although he did not journey to East Anglia until 1754, he then made visits on a regular basis, usually once each year, but sometimes more often. Many towns and villages in Norfolk and Suffolk saw something of the diminutive preacher and, over the years spanning his excursions, large numbers of Methodist societies were established.

All the places which John Wesley visited in Norfolk and Suffolk and which are recorded in his journal are listed here. Some of them saw him again and again, others just once. Some heard many sermons whilst other places seem to have had a transitory stop only.

The ongoing story of these Methodist societies constitutes a rich history, but the record of them in this book does not explore that history beyond John Wesley's death in March 1791.

*A milestone on the turnpike road from
Thetford to Norwich*

Introduction

In high summer of the year 1754, John Wesley and several others rode through East Anglia on their way to Lakenham just outside the city of Norwich. It was John Wesley's first visit to the region and during the next thirty-seven years he would make more than forty further visits, the last within a few months of his death in 1791.

John Wesley, a priest in the Church of England, had been encouraged by his friend, the evangelist George Whitefield, to try preaching in the open air just as he himself had begun to do. Wesley reluctantly agreed and addressed a crowd of 3000 in a brickfield not far from Bristol in April 1739 with great success. Convinced that in this way he could reach the unchurched, he continued to preach where ever he could, his endeavours becoming part of 'the great awakening' emerging in various parts of the country.

John Wesley's genius lay in his organisational ability. He quickly saw that it was vital to support his followers and nurture them in the religious life. Consequently, he gathered his hearers and converts into local groups or 'societies' with a universal set of rules and practices, although he always insisted that his societies were designed to provide spiritual leaven within the Church of England and should remain within the Anglican communion. These societies were clustered into circuits, the circuits into Districts and the whole into the Methodist Connexion, with its annual Conference, an organisational arrangement which exists to this day.

It was not pure chance that John Wesley visited Norwich at this time. He was always anxious that his energies were used to maximum effect. Consequently, he tended to visit places where he could reach the largest number of people. London, Bristol, Newcastle were places he visited often, but he failed to come to Norwich in the earlier years, despite it being almost equal in importance to Bristol at this time with both cities only surpassed by London in prominence. It is unclear why Wesley should not have visited Norwich in the 1740s. It is also unclear why Norwich should have been listed as one of the Methodist circuits in 1749 when no evidence appears to exist of Methodist activity in the city. However, a sequence of events which began in 1751, made it almost impossible for him to visit the city for the following few years.

From the beginning of his preaching ministry, John Wesley assembled a group of men who were ready to accept his leadership in their attempts to awaken, strengthen and deepen the spiritual lives of all who heard them

Timberhill and Hog Hill

OS TG 235085

Thursday 1 August 1754 - The hill was covered with drunkards and rioters: but we saw the hand of God turning them aside and keeping them at a distance...The congregation looked like sheep in the midst of wolves...[2]

Tuesday 6 August 1754 - I preached contrary to my design on the hill. The rioters were there in great numbers. I called them to repentance, but they stopped their ears and ran upon me, casting dirt and stones etc. I stood it for three-quarters of an hour; but it was fighting with beasts...Our people were a good deal discouraged, fearing it will grow worse and worse...[3]

Friday 9 August 1754 –At six a tumultuous crowd surrounded me while I cried aloud 'Let the wicked forsake his way and the unrighteous man his thoughts.[4]

* * * * * * *

For the first few days, Charles Wesley's preaching was heard by a quiet and well behaved crowd of listeners. About a thousand people gathered to hear the open-air sermons. Several clergymen were in the crowd on one occasion as well as a couple of Justices of the Peace. Perhaps these two were present in order to judge whether or not the occasions were orderly. However, this peace did not last.

Timberhill was a rough and violent thoroughfare running down from Ber Street to the Bell Inn and the Gardener's Arms public houses[5] at the lower end. Here the street widened into a triangular area known in the eighteenth century as Hog Hill. It could provide room for people to gather and listen to Charles Wesley's sermons in 1754, but its drawbacks were the two public houses on either side of the street. Here, there were plenty of troublemakers ready to disrupt the congregations. Further interruptions came from the many butchers with their slaughter houses based in Ber Street whom Charles noted were constantly passing to and fro whilst he was preaching although they were quiet at first. On one occasion, Charles recorded in his diary that those drinking in one of the inns persuaded some butchers to disturb the service. *In the last hymn, they made up to the table with great*

---

[2] *The Life of the Rev. Charles Wesley.* Thomas Jackson, London, 18 41, vol. ii, p.53 [hereafter *Life*].
[3] Ibid., p.56.
[4] Ibid., p.57.
[5] The Gardener's Arms is now called the Murderer's Arms public house.

fury. The foremost often lifted up his stick to strike me, being within his reach; but he was not permitted.[6]

Fortunately for Charles, a safer preaching place was offered him and instead of the open street, he addressed the crowds in the nearby Lamb Inn Yard. He estimated that when the yard was filled with hearers, more people could stand at the lower part of Hog Hill and still hear what was being said.[7]

Charles Wesley – engraved by T.A. Dean

Timberhill had also seen much violence against James Wheatley and his followers. He, too, had chosen to preach here when he had first come to the city in 1751 and had been beset by continual violence from the mob, far greater than Charles Wesley experienced three years later. In addition to the Bell and the Gardener's Arms, the Squirrel, another public house in

---

[6] *Life...,* Jackson, op. cit., p.54.
[7] In 1900, a road was cut through this area to make a way for trams.

16

Timberhill, was frequented by the rioters who had attacked James Wheatley's services.

One of the residents of the parish of St John Timberhill was the widow, Dorothy Overton. She lived at the top of the hill near to its junction with Golden Ball Street and the church of St John and it was on a piece of her ground that James Wheatley's first wooden Tabernacle building had been erected. It was quickly destroyed by rioters who untiled the building and sawed through its upright timbers thus making it unusable. In addition they attacked Dorothy Overton and her daughter with considerable violence, covering both of them with mud from head to foot.

Dorothy Overton had continued to support Wheatley and was a member of his congregation until the rumours of his scandalous sexual behaviour began to circulate. At that point, said Charles Wesley, *sin forced her out*[8] and she left the Tabernacle.

In the summer of 1754, she attended the preaching of Charles Wesley and shortly afterwards she offered herself as a candidate for the Methodist society. In consequence, the Tabernacle congregation was *above measure displeased with her. She regards it not, but follows on to know the Lord.*[9]

The Bell Hotel

OS TG 235085

Wednesday 24 July 1754 – My congregation at night was considerably increased by the market-folk out of the country…Towards the close, a huge man tried to ride up to me, but the people interposed again and again, till a serious stout man took and led his horse away and kept the poor drunkard at a due distance. Some in the public house behind me were noisy and troublesome…[10]

Friday 2 August 1754 - I stood under a window of the Bell. Satan quickly sent me two of his drunken champions who did all in their power to interrupt me.[11]

---

[8] *Life…*, Jackson, op, cit., p.54.
[9] Ibid., p.58.
[10] Ibid., p.51.
[11] Ibid., p.53.

Saturday 3 August 1754 – It being a fair-day, we had a large company of drunkards to wait upon us at seven.[12]

* * * * * * *

The Bell Hotel
with the open area known as Hog Hill on the left of the picture

Also known as the Blue Bell, this coaching inn at the bottom of Timberhill was well-known for its cock-fighting matches. It was also the meeting place of the Hell Fire Club in the middle years of the eighteenth century. This group of well-to-do 'gentlemen' amused themselves by paying small sums to violent individuals, encouraging them to attack those who gathered to hear John and Charles Wesley's preaching.

Mr Edwards' House

OS TG 234085

Mr Edwards must have been personally acquainted with the Wesley brothers for he met them and their companions on their journey at Attleborough and accompanied them to Lakenham where they were to stay

---

[12] Ibid.

at the home of Captain and Mrs Gallatin. A Norwich bookseller, Mr Edwards owned a house and business in the Lamb Inn Yard, *next door*, as he described it, *to the Lamb Back-Gate.*[13]

A year before the arrival of the Wesley brothers, Edwards had advertised in the *Norwich Mercury* on 14 July 1753 to inform the readers that at his premises he had available,

> *the WORKS of the Rev. Mr JOHN WESLEY, M.A. viz. sermons bound and stitch'd, Psalms and Hymns bound and stitch'd, Forms of Prayer, Family Prayers, Instructions for Children, Lessons for Children, together with his Appeals and Journals, and various other Tracts to [sic] tedious to insert. A Catalogue of the whole to be seen at the above Place, with the Price fix'd to each Book.*

Such a comprehensive collection of Methodist books in Norwich at this time suggests close and lengthy contact with the Wesleys for some good time before their arrival in the city.

The Lamb Inn Yard in the late twentieth century

During his five weeks' stay in the summer of 1754, Charles sometimes lodged overnight with Mr and Mrs Edwards in the city. He also preached in their house when the weather was too wet to hold services in the open air. At other times, members of the infant Methodist society joined Charles in

---

[13] Letter in the *Norwich Mercury*, 14 July 1753.

the house following the open-air preaching for further instruction and support.

On Thursday 8 August 1754, Charles noted – *Our morning hour is always peaceable and attended with the blessing of the Gospel. The house is filled with the sincere; and the half-awakened listen without.*[14]

The following day, Charles recorded in his journal that James Wheatley had called at the Edwards' house. *Mrs Edwards opened the door and, seeing him, without speaking a word, bad or good, shut it again.*[15]

During the next few years, John Wesley stayed at Mr Edwards' house whenever he was visiting the city.

The Foundery[16]

OS TG 234085

21 July 1754 - The rain hindered my preaching. God is providing us a place, an old large house which the owner, a Justice of the Peace, has reserved for us. He has refused several, always declaring he would let it to none but John Wesley. Last Saturday, Mr Edwards agreed to take a lease for seven years...

23 July 1754 – I met Mr S-----n at the house which is at present a mere heap of rubbish, without walls, roof, floor, doors or windows. What will this chaos produce? I think it no bad omen that this was originally a Foundery[17]

*   *   *   *   *   *   *

The Foundery stood in the Lamb Inn yard. In the thirteenth century, this area bounded by Red Lion Street, White Lion Street and the Haymarket was the Jewish quarter. It was completely destroyed by fire in 1286. A church was built on part of the site. It was eventually converted to an inn and took the name 'The Holy Lamb' or, simply, 'The Lamb.' In addition to the Lamb Inn, the Goose and Gridiron Inn stood here, together with a grand house which had once been the home of Sir Thomas Browne, physician and author, in the seventeenth century and Mr Edwards' house where both Charles and later John stayed whilst in the city.

---

[14] *Life...* , Jackson, op. cit., vol. ii, p.57.
[15] Ibid., p.58.
[16] John and Charles Wesley always spelled the name in this way.
[17] *Life...*, Jackson, op. cit., vol. ii, p.50-1.

Charles, who remained in Norwich in the summer of 1754 after John's departure, searched for a preaching house safe from the attacks and disturbances of the mob and from the ravages of the weather. A Justice of the Peace and City official, John Simpson,[18] who had heard one of the first sermons preached by Charles in Norwich, offered him the lease of the brew house which stood in the same yard. This building had originally been a bell foundry and Charles noted the significance of it having the same name as the Methodist centre in London. It was utterly ruinous. Simpson sent his workmen to repair the building. This clearly was a major task as the premises were not licensed for worship until October 1755.

A small Methodist society of about eighteen members was established while Charles was in the city and a number more gave in their names before he left including one who had belonged to a Methodist society in London and another in Newcastle.

As in a number of other places round the country, it had been Charles Wesley rather than John who had first preached in Norfolk and it was Charles who established the first Methodist society in the county.

In February 1757, John Wesley was pleased to be able to visit the Norwich Methodist society.

> *I had long desired to see the little flock at Norwich, but this I could not decently do till I was able to rebuild part of the Foundery there to which I was engaged by my lease. A sum sufficient for that end was now unexpectedly given me by one of whom I had no personal knowledge. I set out on Monday 28th.*

He arrived in time to preach there on Tuesday evening, the day following, and *after preaching I entered into contract with a builder and gave him part of the money in hand.*[19] The building was to be the home of the Methodists in Norwich for about seven years.

The new Methodist society in Norwich was incorporated into the Methodist system of organisation. As other Methodist congregations were established in Norfolk, Suffolk and part of Essex, they were gathered into the huge Norwich circuit.

From the autumn of 1754, itinerant Methodist preachers were stationed in the city. The first was Samuel Larwood who had been sent to Norwich by the Wesleys the previous year. In the earlier years, preachers were

---

[18] He was a glover by trade and held various public posts in the city. He was Sheriff in 1755.

[19] *The Journal of the Rev. John Wesley. A.M.*, ed. Nehemiah Curnock, 1909-16, London, vol. iv, pp.197-8.

moved on every two months. This was extended to four months in 1758, but the drawbacks of such an arrangement soon led to a further change so that by the 1760s a year had become the usual time allotted. In 1784, the maximum length of service in any one circuit was extended to three years.

When John Wesley took over the lease of the Tabernacle, he wrote of the contrast between the difficult and headstrong Tabernacle congregation and the disciplined, settled congregation at the Foundery. In 1759, after preaching at the Foundery, he wrote, *how pleasing it would be to flesh and blood to remain in this quiet place.*[20]

The Foundery building was given up sometime after in 1761 and the congregation joined that at the Tabernacle at St Martin-at-Palace Plain.

The Tabernacle

OS TG 236092

The Tabernacle on St Martin-at-Palace Plain, built in 1752-3, was planned by Thomas Ivory, the Norwich architect who also designed the Octagon Chapel and the Assembly House. This Tabernacle was the second building of that name. The first was a wooden building at the top of Timberhill which had been used by James Wheatley and his congregation and which had been attacked and destroyed by the mob in 1751.

Money was collected amongst those who were attracted to Wheatley's preaching and was added to a considerable donation from the Countess of Huntingdon. It was used to build this very substantial chapel which could seat about a thousand people. The evangelist and friend of the Wesleys, George Whitefield, was invited to conduct the official opening of the Tabernacle in April 1753. He described the event in his journal, writing that *the polite and great seemed to hear with great attention.*[21] The new chapel created a considerable stir of interest and Whitefield informed a correspondent, *For these three days past, I have been preaching here twice a day ... and, I believe, hundreds of truly awakened souls attend. What*

---

[20] Ibid., p.301.

[21] *The Life and Times of Selina, Countess of Huntingdon* by a Member of the Houses of Shirley and Hastings, 1840, London, vol. i, p.336.

cannot GOD do?[22] Again on the following day, his enthusiasm continued; *In spite of all opposition, he hath caused us to triumph even in Norwich.*[23]

The Tabernacle was built of brick with a pantile roof. It had sash windows and a plain doorway with a heavy lintel. Inside, there was a gallery. The chapel cost £1530, a huge sum at that time, as well as £230 for the land. Once the chapel was completed, Thomas Ivory built a house for James Wheatley. It stood at right angles to one end of the Tabernacle and next to the road. The house was a beautiful building of three storeys with sash windows and a shallow flight of stone steps up to the front door.

As the legal process against him gathered force, Wheatley withdrew from the Tabernacle. The congregation then quarrelled repeatedly over the question as to who would minister to them. In the event, the task was taken on principally by preachers from George Whitefield's Tabernacle in Moorfields in London.

In August 1755, George Whitefield was invited by the Countess of Huntingdon and Major and Mrs Gallatin to re-open the Tabernacle after Wheatley's disgrace. That the Gallatins should have urged this visit is a little surprising in view of Wesley's hostility to Calvinism. Indeed, it is clear that Wesley strongly disapproved of Whitefield's support for what Wesley saw as a rival congregation to his own at the Foundery. Whitefield wrote to Wesley insisting that he had come to Norwich simply to advance the glory of God, that his time was too precious to waste in vindicating himself against those informers who wished to make trouble and that he would see John Wesley the following week when they should then have the opportunity to talk face to face.

George Whitefield saw the re-opening of the Tabernacle as a great success. He wrote to a friend saying that *a glorious work* had begun at the Tabernacle *and is now carrying on.*[24] This was in spite of the fact that the case against Wheatley was being heard in the Norwich Consistory Court. It seems that in spite of the charges against Wheatley and the widespread knowledge of his scandalous behaviour, George Whitefield and the Countess of Huntingdon were not slow in lending the Tabernacle their support and that large congregations were never wanting.

Finally Wheatley was condemned for immorality after a prolonged legal process in which his appeals against the sentence were rejected. Then he

---

[22] *The Work of the Rev. George Whitefield, MA*, London, 1771, vol. iii, Letters 1753-70, letter dccccclxxi, 17 April 1753, reprinted Quinta Press, 2000.

[23] Ibid., letter dccccclxxii, 18 April 1753.

[24] Ibid., vol. i, p.336.

left Norwich in disgrace. Before he went away in 1759, he offered the lease of the Tabernacle to John Wesley who hesitated for a while and eventually agreed to take it over. He believed that 'the hand of God' was behind his action. However when he next visited Norwich just a few weeks later, he found the congregations at the Tabernacle had *mouldered into nothing. Of the fifteen or sixteen hundred subscribers, not twenty, not one, was left.*[25]

The Tabernacle with the minister's house on the left

It is unclear why Wheatley should have offered the lease of the Tabernacle to John Wesley, an opponent on theological grounds and one who had made it clear even before he came to Norwich that he wanted nothing to do with Wheatley or his congregation at the Tabernacle. It would have been far more appropriate to have offered the lease to the Countess of Huntingdon with her brand of Calvinistic Methodism especially as she had given so much money towards the building. George Whitefield, the Countess' colleague and friend, who had preached at the Tabernacle on several memorable occasions, might also have been an

---

[25] Curnock, op. cit., vol. iv, p.301.

appropriate lessee or, indeed, even William Cudworth who had set up his own small connexion of meetings in London and who regularly ministered to the congregation at the Tabernacle. As it was, Wesley's decision to take on the building and congregation was an unfortunate misjudgement and one which caused continual vexation for him.

It was clear that the preachers at the Tabernacle had warned the congregation against Wesley and his theological views. Undeterred, John Wesley took the matter in hand and began to organise the congregation on Methodist lines. *I desired that those who were willing to join in a society would speak with me the next evening. About twenty did so; but the greater part of these appeared like frightened sheep; and no marvel, when they had been so long accustomed to hear all manner of evil of me.*[26] On subsequent days, more people applied to join the society, but over the years Wesley had endless trouble with the Calvinist congregation. He told them *they were the most ignorant self-conceited, self-willed, fickle, intractable, disorderly, disjointed society in the Three Kingdoms.*[27] He repeatedly reproved them for their behaviour, their failure to adhere to Methodist practice and he battled with their doubtful religious opinions. John Murlin, one of the Methodist itinerant preachers at the Tabernacle at this time wrote, *Many of Wheatley's dear lambs were little better than wolves.*[28] The number of members fluctuated wildly.

As well as repeated troubles within the congregation, the mob often disturbed services and vandalism was also a constant problem. John Pawson, who was stationed in the city as a preacher in 1764, wrote of his ministry in the city.

> *During the winter we had almost continual mobbing. The rioters frequently broke the windows, interrupted us in preaching, and abused the people when service was ended. We made complaint to the mayor, but he would not do us justice; which encouraged the rioters, and led them to commit still greater outrages.*[29]

At one time, an effigy of a preacher was carried about the streets and burned in the parish of St Augustine. The wildness and disorder was

---

[26] Ibid.
[27] Ibid., vol. iv, p.351.
[28] When Wheatley had first preached in Norwich, his supporters were nicknamed his 'dear lambs' and the name stuck.
[29] *Arminian Magazine*, London, 1779, p.38.

calmed only by the intervention of Henry Gurney, the Quaker banker, whose premises were situated in that part of the city.

When the lease ran out in 1765, Wesley relinquished Methodist supervision there with great relief. The stubborn and difficult congregation at the Tabernacle contrasted starkly with the peaceable and tractable Methodist congregation which had met at the Foundery.

After John Wesley relinquished the Tabernacle, Wheatley eventually leased the chapel to the Countess of Huntingdon for the use of her Connexion and after his death in 1775, the Countess bought the building. She and a companion, Lady Anne Erskine, visited Norwich in the following spring. Augustus Toplady, the stout defender of Calvinism and bitter theological controversialist, was also one of the party and during his stay in the city, he preached at the Tabernacle.[30]

In a letter a few months later, the Countess wrote of the success of the Tabernacle; *I have one congregation at Norwich, four thousand hearers, six hundred communicants and this, under two students who write me word that about thirty were added to that society in three weeks.*[31]

A series of gifted young preachers ministered at the Tabernacle. One of these was Mr Shirley, a relative of the Countess, grandson of the first Earl Ferrars and brother of the fourth, fifth and sixth Earls. His appointment was greeted with enormous curiosity in Norwich and many from the upper and middle classes flocked to hear him preach at the Tabernacle. Mr Shirley's appointment marked the highest point of the popularity of the chapel. Thereafter, a series of disputes, fractures and defections amongst the congregation led to a slow and inexorable decline.[32]

Norwich Cathedral

O S TG 236089

Sunday 18 January 1761 – I met the society in the morning and many of them went with me to the Cathedral.[33]

*   *   *   *   *   *   *

---

[30] He had written his best-known hymn, 'Rock of Ages....' in the previous year.
[31] *The Life and Times of Selina...*, op. cit., vol. i, p.343.
[32] In 1918, the chapel building was taken over by the British Gas Light Company and was turned into a garage. The building was demolished in 1953. More recently, the derelict graveyard has been made into a public garden.
[33] Curnock, op. cit., vol. iv, p.431.

John Wesley was insistent that Methodists should attend the services in Anglican churches. He stressed that Methodism should act as a leaven to intensify spirituality within the church. He had no intention that Methodists should separate themselves from the Church of England and become dissenters.

Initially no Methodist services were held during the times of Anglican services so that members could attend their own parish churches and John Wesley set an example by taking his congregations to church with him and often when he was in Norwich he went *as usual to the Cathedral.*[34] Charles Wesley attended the Cathedral during his stay in Norwich in the summer of 1754 and received communion from the hands of Bishop Thomas Hayter.[35] There were only twenty people who received communion that Sunday morning.

However, as time went by, this practice of holding Methodist services outside Anglican service hours was relaxed. Many who joined the Methodist societies had never been active members of the Church of England and regarded themselves as wholly separate from it. They had no interest, therefore, in attending Anglican services.

The site of the Tabernacle was just to the north-east of the Cathedral and so it was only a brief walk from there into the Close.

The Octagon

OS TG 232091

Wednesday 23 November 1757 – I was shown Dr Taylor's new meeting-house, perhaps the most elegant one in Europe. It is eight-square, built of the finest brick, with sixteen sash windows below, as many above, and eight sky-lights in the dome, which, indeed, are purely ornamental. The inside is finished in the highest taste, and is as clean as any nobleman's saloon. The communion-table is fine mahogany; the very latches of the pew-doors are polished brass. How can it be thought that the old, coarse gospel should find admission here?[36]

*   *   *   *   *   *   *

---

[34] Ibid., vol.v, p.100.
[35] Thomas Hayter (1702-62) was Bishop of Norwich from 1749-61. He then became Bishop of London.
[36] Curnock, op. cit., vol. iv, p.244.

Built for the Presbyterians[37] in 1754-6 by the distinguished Norwich architect, Thomas Ivory, the Octagon displayed a high degree of architectural sophistication. Its eight-sided design greatly pleased John Wesley and he strongly advocated that Methodist preaching houses should be built according to this pattern. As a result, fourteen Methodist octagons were built around the country.

The Norwich Octagon is situated in the parish of St George, Colegate, then the wealthiest part of the city. It attracted many adherents from the upper echelons of Norwich society.

The Octagon Chapel, Norwich
from a drawing by James Sillett 1828

It is a grand chapel with an octagonal roof. The pillared and pedimented portico of the main entrance fronts a flight of shallow steps. Inside the chapel are eight huge Corinthian columns with galleries running between them and a wooden backboard behind the pulpit. It cost the enormous sum of £5000 which was raised by the congregation itself.

In spite of Wesley's somewhat critical eye regarding the Octagon's opulence, he was impressed by its architectural merit and even after all his

---

[37] By 1820 the congregation had changed its allegiance and become Unitarian.

years of travel, John Wesley still claimed in 1787 that the Octagon in Norwich *is the most elegant I ever saw.*[38]

It is, perhaps, a telling remark that the Octagon was kept clean and one wonders how clean chapels and meeting-houses usually were in the eighteenth century.

Dr John Taylor, the minister at the Octagon at the time of its building, was a renowned Hebrew scholar. John Wesley's view was that John Taylor was a dangerous Calvinist and, worse, a heretic, diverging significantly from gospel truth. Wesley's efforts to refute Taylor's opinions were all the more fervent for, as Wesley noted in his journal, whenever Dr Taylor's opinions were influential, Wesley's own preaching made no impression. Taylor's book on the doctrine of original sin[39] was refuted by Wesley's own carefully-argued book on the subject and the two men corresponded on the subject for some time. Yet they never spoke face to face. When Wesley visited the Octagon, John Taylor had already left the city to become tutor at Warrington Dissenting Academy.[40]

St Peter Mancroft

OS TG 229084

Saturday 5 November 1758 – We went to St Peter's church, the Lord's Supper being administered there. I scarcely ever remember to have seen a more beautiful parish church; the more so because its beauty results not from foreign ornaments, but from the very form and structure of it. It is very large and of an uncommon height and the sides are almost all window, so that it has an awful and venerable look and, at the same time, surprisingly cheerful.[41]

*   *   *   *   *   *   *

Presumably this description is of the church of St Peter Mancroft rather than one of the three other Norwich churches dedicated to St Peter.

---

[38] Curnock, op. cit., vol. vii, p.287.
[39] John Taylor's book *The Scriptural Doctrine of Original Sin* was published in 1740. The book then went through several editions. John Taylor 1694-1761.
[40] For further reading, see *Wesley's Arch-Heretic*, Geoffrey Thackeray Eddy, 2003, Epworth Press.
[41] Curnock, op. cit., vol. iv, p.290-1.

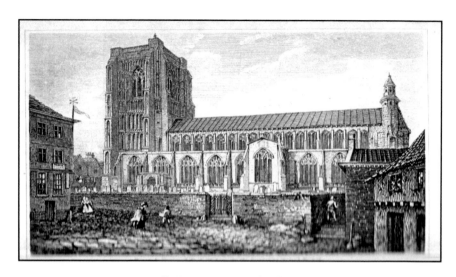

St Peter Mancroft Church

This great fifteenth-century perpendicular church stands at one side of the market place facing the mediaeval Guildhall on the other side. Its soaring west tower with corner turrets[42] looks out over the castle ditches to the great keep on the opposite hill. It contains a wall plaque commemorating the doctor and author, Sir Thomas Browne. It had a splendid organ in Wesley's time. It was the largest parish church in Norwich and it was also the city's richest parish church with the incumbent receiving an annual stipend of £100 in the later eighteenth century. It was only a short walk through the market place to St Peter Mancroft church for Wesley and the Foundery congregation meeting in the Lamb Inn Yard.

Charles Wesley attended worship at this church when he was in the city at the end of July 1754.

The Priory

OS TG 235095

Thursday 16 January 1766 – I rode to Norwich and preached at seven in a large place called 'The Priory.' The room, I suppose, was formerly the chapel; I like it the better on that account. After spending three days here

---

[42] The spire was added in 1895.

more agreeably than I had done for many years, on Monday the 20th I left a Society of a hundred and seventy members, regular and well-united together.[43]

*   *   *   *   *   *   *

Once the lease of the Tabernacle had expired in 1765, it became imperative for the Methodists to find a new meeting place.

The General Baptists were asked for the use of their chapel. Initially this request was not welcomed as the Baptist meeting-house and the minister's house had suffered from broken windows whilst the mob was rioting against James Wheatley. Although they twice declined to hire it out to the Methodists, the request was finally granted in the hope that it *may be a means to make them entertain a better and more favourable opinion of us and our principles and practice.* They hoped, too, that the Methodists would attend their services and so *enlighten their minds...*[44]

This chapel had been part of the mediaeval buildings of the White Friars' complex near St James' Church[45] to the north of the Cathedral.

The Priory was the home of Norwich Methodists for two-and-a-half years.

Cherry Lane Chapel

OS TG 230095

Sunday 1 November 1772 – In the evening, many hundreds went away, not being able to squeeze into the room. For those that were within, it was a blessed season.[46]

*   *   *   *   *   *   *

The meeting room at the Priory soon proved far too small for the Methodist congregation. When John Wesley was in Norwich in February 1769 he administered communion to 170 Methodists at the Priory in the

---

[43] Curnock, op. cit., vol. v, p.153.

[44] *The Baptists in Norfolk*, C.B. Jewson, 1957, London, p.53.

[45] Unfortunately, Nehemiah Curnock, in his edition of the journal of John Wesley, wrongly identified this chapel as being part of the Blackfriars' church on St Andrew's Plain and the recent edition of John Wesley's journal in *The Works of John Wesley*, ed. W. Reginald Ward and Richard P. Heitzenrater, Nashville, 1993, vol, 22, p.29 fn, has copied this error.

[46] Curnock, op. cit., vol. v, p.487.

morning, but when he came to preach in the evening, he found that as *the house would not contain one-third of the congregation, I was obliged to stand in the open air – a sight which has not been seen at Norwich for many years.*[47]

It was clear that with the rapidly increasing congregation, the need for larger premises was imperative and the Methodists began to feel that they were now strong enough to build their own chapel. John Wesley wrote to Charles, *I am preparing to build at Norwich; for no place already built can be procured for love or money.*[48] However, hostility to their cause was still in evidence, fanned by their oblique association with James Wheatley and his shameful behaviour, and this made the search for a suitable plot extremely difficult.

Eventually, a parcel of land was secured in the parish of St George, Colegate by John Perowne, one of the Norwich Methodists and a twisterer[49] and shopkeeper by trade.[50] It was situated in Cherry Lane, just off Pitt Street, between Pelican Yard and Adelaide Yard and was next to the Cherry Tree public house. The stone-laying ceremony took place early in 1769 with the foundation stone laid by the itinerant preachers then stationed in Norwich, Duncan Wright and Alexander McNab. The chapel with galleries and box pews as well as a house for the preachers was quickly built. The house was of an unusual design, for a heavy central door at its front opened into a covered passageway leading to the chapel at the rear. This door could be closed at the times of services in order to protect the congregation from any disturbance.

Wesley himself contributed £270 of the building costs whilst £73.5.9d was allocated from Connexional funds in order to reduce the remaining debts on the building.

John Wesley travelled to Norwich at the end of October 1769 with a group of companions. He performed the opening ceremony at the chapel and then *preached in the shell of the new house, crowded enough both within and without.*[51] It seems that the building was not yet completely finished.

---

[47] Ibid., pp.302-3.
[48] *The Letters of the Rev. John Wesley*, ed. John Telford, London, 1931, vol. iv, p.277 (hereafter *Letters*).
[49] A twisterer was someone employed in the weaving industry whose job was to twist together the end of a new length of yarn with the end of that already woven.
[50] John Perowne also registered properties for worship in Winfarthing, King's Lynn and Great Ellingham.
[51] Curnock, op. cit., vol. v, p.347.

*The Preachers' house with its central door leading to
Cherry Lane Chapel*

The chapel keeper was Mary Porter. She had been one of the first members at the Foundery. In 1777, she became chapel keeper at Cherry Lane where she was *distinguished for her kindness and attention to the comfort of the Preachers, by whom she was respected as a mother.*[52]

Congregations fluctuated during the 1770s as a result of a series of disputes, but from 1777 the congregations grew once again and within two years, John Wesley was again complaining that *the new chapel was far too small in the evening. I suppose many hundreds went away.*[53]

In a lecture given in 1876, Dr Thomas Stoughton described his memories of Norwich many years before. He had attended Cherry Lane Chapel as a small boy and recalled that his mother had told him that in the 1770s, the congregation was sometimes disturbed *by young fellows coming in to the evening service and bringing with them birds which they would let fly, that by the fluttering of their wings, they might extinguish the few tallow candles.*[54]

---

[52] *Wesleyan Magazine*, 1822, p.225.
[53] Ibid., p.436.
[54] 'Dr Stoughton's Lecture,' Jack Burton, in *Wesley Historical Society, East Anglia Journal*, 102, Summer 2005.

Members of the congregation at Cherry Lane were often troubled by disorder levelled against them. On Saturday 2 December 1775, for example, John Wesley recorded in his journal that,

> *in the evening a large mob gathered at the door of the preaching-house, the captain of which struck many (chiefly women) with a large stick. Mr Randall,* [the itinerant preacher] *going out to see what was the matter, he struck him with it in the face. But he was soon secured and carried before the mayor, who knowing him to be a notorious offender, against whom one or two warrants were then lying, sent him to jail without delay.*[55]

John Wesley visited the Norwich Methodists almost every year up to and including 1790, shortly before his death in March 1791. He usually lodged with the preachers in their house which was set conveniently just in front of the chapel. He noted in his journal that when he preached at half past five in the afternoon, it was *to as many as the house would contain; and even those that could not get in stayed more quiet and silent than ever I saw them before.*[56]

The death of Wesley was received with great sorrow amongst the Norwich Methodists. They flocked to Cherry Lane Chapel to hear a moving funeral sermon for their 'father in God' whom many would have known and loved.[57]

Ber Street

'*Monday 1 November 1784 ...at Dr Hunt's, dinner within...*'[58]

*   *   *   *   *   *   *

John Hunt, who was Wesley's host on this and other occasions, lived in Ber Street, Norwich. He was a surgeon and practised his profession in the city.

For many years he was a Methodist local preacher. He joined the Methodists after a colourful denominational career. In his obituary in the

---

[55] Curnock, op. cit., vol.vi, pp.86-7.
[56] Ibid., p.133.
[57] The Methodists built a larger chapel in Calvert Street in 1811 and in 1818 Cherry Lane Chapel was sold to the Baptists who renamed it 'Providence.' It was demolished in 1936.
[58] Curnock, op. cit., vol. vi, p.29.

Norfolk Chronicle[59] he was described as having allied himself at various times with the Presbyterians, Independents, Baptists, Swedenborgians and Unitarians as well as attending his parish church before he finally becoming a Methodist.

In January 1781, he had applied for and obtained from the bishop a licence for religious worship for a summer house in his garden. This was then used for services and John Wesley mentioned preaching there in 1781 and 1783. The chapel was known as 'Ebenezer' chapel.[60]

Wesley commended the Ber Street congregation. In a letter to Jonathan Coussins, the Norwich Assistant[61] in 1785, he wrote, *Dr Hunt and his people shame us; I mean in fasting which we have well-nigh forgotten! Let us begin again!*[62]

One of the itinerant preachers, Thomas Cooper, who was stationed in the Norwich circuit in 1782, remembered that he had been taken ill *by a putrid fever* and felt,

> *there was not the least prospect of my recovery...Mr Hunt, a most skilful surgeon and a truly pious man, who was my medical attendant, with strong cries and prayers, pleaded with God to rebuke the disorder...The Lord in mercy heard and answered...by giving the healing touch; for I improved in my help from that very hour; and my kind surgeon, though he attended me for a long time, and with great assiduity, never made any charge, only requesting me to preach to him a sermon, which I cheerfully did as soon as I was able.*[63]

Hunt was described as *a man of extraordinary piety and extensive benevolence.*[64] On at least two occasions, he provided a banquet for the poor. The first was reported in the *Norwich Mercury* newspaper which recorded that *110 persons as belonging to St John de Sepulchre in this city received a comfortable dinner of dumplings, beef etc from Mr Hunt,*

[59] *Norfolk Chronicle*, 3 July 1824.
[60] In 1806, a controversy amongst the Norwich Methodists led to a split in the congregation. The smaller group broke away and joined Ebenezer Chapel. Preachers were invited there from the Methodist New Connexion.
[61] 'Assistant' was the title of the supervising minister in each circuit. After John Wesley's death, it was changed to 'Superintendent.'
[62] *Letters....*Telford, op. cit., vol. vii, p.259 – letter 25 Feb. 1785.
[63] *Wesleyan Methodist Magazine*, 1835, p.41.
[64] *Norfolk Annals*, ed. Charles Mackie, 1901. vol. i, p.235 quoting the *Norfolk and Norwich Remembrancer*.

surgeon.[65] The second of these feasts was held to celebrate the news of the recovery of King George III from his illness and his return to normality.

During his visits to Norwich in October 1783, John Wesley was entertained by John Hunt at his house in Ber Street and he was again at Dr Hunt's house at the beginning of November the following year and once more eleven months later. He was there twice more in the autumn of 1786 for meals, conversation and prayers.

John Hunt remained a committed Methodist in Norwich for many years, but eventually retired to Gissing in south Norfolk. His name appeared as a local preacher on the preaching plan for the Diss Methodist Circuit in 1814 and he made a number of financial donations to the circuit. At Gissing he founded a chapel 'made up of a heterogeneous mixture of doctrines.'[66] In his will, he left this chapel to be administered by four trustees and directed that it should be for the use of the Methodist preachers whenever they were able to visit. He died on 16 June 1824 aged 86.

St Augustine's Church

O S TG 228096

Sunday 5 October 1788 – Sunday the 5th was a comfortable day ...7 am administered the Lord's Supper and at two in the afternoon and six in the evening when I preached to very serious congregations. Diary - 10.30 St Aug[ustine]

*   *   *   *   *   *   *

On this occasion, John Wesley had given communion to the members at Cherry Lane Chapel immediately before taking the congregation to the parish church of St Augustine for morning worship. For a while, administering communion had been a controversial issue in Norwich. Whilst James Wheatley had been in charge of the Tabernacle, he had given communion to his congregation there although he was not an ordained minister. When Wesley took over the lease of the Tabernacle, the Methodist preachers in the city followed the Methodist practice and encouraged their members to attend the Anglican church for this purpose.

---

[65] *Norwich Mercury*, 27 January 1781.
[66] *Norfolk Annals*, op. cit., p.235.

Problems, however, arose. Some Anglican clergy refused to give communion to Methodists. In addition, the Tabernacle congregation had become used to regular communion services and were resentful when Wesley insisted on Methodist practice. He noted that large numbers of the congregation ceased attending services because of this rule.

In 1760, it became known throughout the Connexion that the three Norwich preachers, James Glazebrook, Paul Greenwood and Isaac Brown had made a decision to provide communion for their members. It is possible that they were not taking such a uniquely innovative step for John Murlin, another itinerant preacher, later claimed that when he had been stationed in Norwich in 1756, he had regularly administered communion. This was in complete contrast to Methodist instructions

Although Wesley believed that ordination was essential for this practice, he decided to leave the matter to the next meeting of Conference. Charles Wesley, in contrast to his brother's calm approach, was highly angered and threatened to leave the Methodist movement if it was not forbidden. Matters were resolved at the 1760 Conference when Wesley asserted that the call to preach did not give the right to administer the sacrament and this was accepted by the preachers.

St Augustine's Church, Norwich

The incumbent of St Augustine's, when answering the Bishop's questions in the 1784 Visitation, mentioned the Cherry Lane meeting house and said it was *resorted to by inferior people.* He complained that there were too many Dissenters in every parish of the City especially amongst the lowest class, but acknowledged that *the more orderly of this Class are very many of them followers of the Methodists.*[67]

Cherry Lane Chapel was very close to St Augustine's and the two churches almost faced each other across Pitt Street. They stood a little way inside the northern section of the city wall near St Augustine's Gate.[68] In the eighteenth century this was still an open area of fields and gardens.

St Augustine's Church is a modest flint building. The church boasts a tower of brick which was a 1682-7 replacement of the original flint tower, the remains of which can be seen in the bottom few feet.

St George's Church

O S TG 230091

Sunday 17 October 1790 - ...we went to our own parish church although there was no sermon there, nor at any of the thirty-six churches in the town, save the cathedral and St Peter's.[69]

*   *   *   *   *   *   *

Cherry Lane Chapel was situated at the north end of the parish of St George, Colegate and was much nearer to the church of St Augustine. Nevertheless on this occasion John Wesley chose to attend morning worship at St George's, a long walk especially for an old man of 87.

Colegate was a wealthy parish not far from the Cathedral and one which contained two major centres of dissenting worship. One was the Old Meeting for Independents and the other the Octagon for Presbyterians. St Mary Baptist Church was also nearby.[70]

The church of St George was mainly a later fifteenth-century building. It contained a splendid collection of funerary monuments, many of them erected during the course of the eighteenth century, decorated with

---

[67] NRO VIS 29a/7.
[68] St Augustine's Gate was demolished in 1794.
[69] Curnock, op. cit., vol. viii, p.107.
[70] The future Calvert Street Methodist Church which was opened in 1811 was also situated in this parish.

medallions, urns, cherubs, stone drapery, scrolls and other fashionable devices. Many were dedicated to the merchants and city officials who had resided in the parish in their lifetimes, one of whom was Timothy Balderson.[71] He had been city mayor in 1751 when James Wheatley had come to Norwich and it was Balderson who had dealt with the rioting and also with the rioters as he had been the presiding judge at the City Quarter Sessions. His tombstone stated that he had been *a worthy Magistrate.*

It is interesting that John Wesley declares that there was no sermon at this church. The fact that no Anglican sermons were preached in Norwich on this Sunday morning other than the two mentioned, seems a remarkably lax state of affairs in the diocese. Yet the replies of the Norwich clergy to the printed questions sent round by the Bishop in his 1784 'Visitation' indicated that although almost all the city churches held services every Sunday, their services were often held alternately in the mornings or afternoons on subsequent weeks. Two curates served St George's Church and certainly the replies to the 1784 Visitation show that there at least, a sermon was preached on every Sunday afternoon.

Many of the clergy in Norwich who completed the Visitation questions failed to answer the question about how often they preached sermons which raises suspicions that perhaps this did not often happen. Although it is now believed that the somnolent state of much of the Church of England was not as deep as was once thought, a correspondent to the *Norfolk Chronicle* in 1770 pointed to a dismal view of some of the clergy at this time. He wrote that so many of the young clergy pay too much regard -

> *to the fashionable levity of the present age....To what assembly, playhouse or place of resort can we go, but we meet with numbers of them. How many of them do we see (instead of employing their time to far nobler and worthier purposes) trifling with the younger part of the fair sex.*[72]

The Rev. Richard Tapps who had completed the Visitation return in 1784 complained - *the congregation rather thin on account of the many dissenting Families*[73] so the attendance of a large number of Methodists in the congregation on this particular morning must have swelled the congregation enormously.

---

[71] Timothy Balderson died 2 December 1764.
[72] *Norfolk Chronicle*, 12 May 1770.
[73] NRO VIS 29a/7

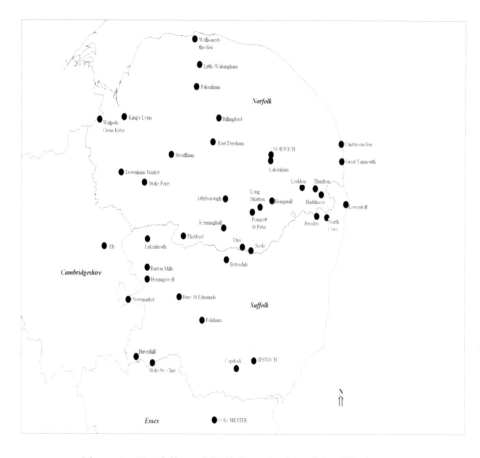

Places in Norfolk and Suffolk visited by John Wesley

Although the focus of John Wesley's first visits to East Anglia was the city of Norwich, he called at many places on his journeys. Other towns and villages attracted his attention and led to visits of enquiry or support for the Methodist Societies already meeting there.

Attleborough

15 miles south-west of Norwich

Monday 8 July 1754 – We were in fear for my brother, lest the heat of the journey should be too great for him, but the rain which God sent down all yesterday had laid the dust and cooled the air.[74]

*   *   *   *   *   *   *

Charles Wesley had set out from London on horseback at four in the morning, together with his friends, Charles Perronet and Robert Windsor and his brother, John. John had been severely ill with what was thought to be consumption and, for a time, had not been expected to live. He was still far from well and very weak, hence the concern Charles felt for him.

The party travelled very slowly so that John would not be exhausted by the journey. Their first stop was at Braintree where they spent the night.

The following day, the four rode on a little beyond Bury St Edmunds. During the course of the journey, John and Charles worked on transcribing and revising their commentary on the New Testament which was published the following year.

> *10 July 1754 – Our leisurely travelling allowed us many hours for writing. Between seven and eight we set out, and by eleven reached Attleborough. Here our brother Edwards met us with a chaise which brought us in the evening to Captain Gallatin's at Lakenham.*[75]

Although John Wesley must have passed through the town on a number of occasions on his journeys to Norwich, Attleborough is not mentioned in his journal. However, the circuit book, the record book kept by the circuit superintendent minister, lists a Methodist society there from 1786.[76] This is the earliest record of Methodism in the town and showed that there were nine members.

---

[74] *Life...*, Jackson, op. cit., vol. ii, p.46.

[75] Ibid.

[76] N.R.O., DIS/DN 16/1, 'The List of the Societies in the Norwich Circuit, 1785-97.' For Captain Gallatin see pp.75-8; for Mr Edwards see pp.18-20.

41

Barton Mills

11 miles north-west of Bury St Edmunds

Tuesday 13 October 1789 – In the evening I went in the mail-coach to Barton Mills...[77]

*   *   *   *   *   *   *

John Wesley had passed through Barton Mills in 1788 when he had travelled there from London via Newmarket in the coach. He had then taken a chaise from Barton Mills in order to visit the Methodists in King's Lynn.

Barton Mills lay at the point at which the road divided, with one arm leading to King's Lynn and the other to Thetford and Norwich.

In 1789, John Wesley again came from London and this time took the late evening mail coach to Barton Mills. There he stayed over night and after breakfast took a chaise to Lynn. In his spare moments on this journey, he read a book called *Irish Antiquities* which he continued to read all week. However, his eyesight was not what it was. Only a few days prior to the East Anglian visit, he had noted in his journal, *My sight is so decayed that I cannot well read by candle-light, but I can write as well as ever.*[78]

There is no evidence of any Methodist society at Barton Mills at this time.

Beccles

17 miles south-east of Norwich
8 miles south-west of Great Yarmouth

Thursday 21 November 1776 – I preached at Beccles. A duller place I have seldom seen. The people of the town were neither pleased nor vexed, as 'caring for none of these things.' Yet fifty or sixty came into the house either to hear or see.[79]

*   *   *   *   *   *   *

[77] Curnock, op. cit., vol. viii, p.18.
[78] Ibid., vol. viii, p.17.
[79] Ibid., vol. vi, p.132.

It was ten years before Wesley was again in the town. Then, he preached to a great crowd, many of whom were unable to squeeze into the meeting-house. In comparison with his previous visit, he found the people there both serious and attentive.

The following year, the Beccles society was recorded in the circuit book as having six members.[80] Although this seems to be a small number, there would have been very many more attenders than just the formal members in the congregation.

Mary Sewell was one of the local preachers who preached at Beccles in the mid 1780s.[81]

Wesley returned to Beccles for a very brief visit in October 1789, arriving there by chaise at 2 pm following lunch at Stubbs Green near Loddon. After a period of prayer with the people gathered to meet him, he left the town just three-quarters of an hour later and returned to Loddon.

Billingford

5 miles north-north-east of East Dereham

Friday 14 August 1761 - We rode to Billingford and on Saturday to Norwich.[82]

*   *   *   *   *   *   *

After preaching and sightseeing at Boston, John Wesley travelled from Lincolnshire to Norfolk in the summer of 1761. He stayed overnight at the very small village of Billingford although there is no record of where he stayed or that he preached there. However, he was accustomed to preach at each place where he spent the night, both in the evening of his arrival and again the following morning at five o'clock and so he may well have done so here.

Before the turnpike road between King's Lynn and Norwich was made in 1770, the main route for travellers lay through Grimston, Litcham, Mileham, North Elmham, Billingford and Attlebridge.

Billingford had been a junction on the Roman road system. One route ran east-west across Norfolk here and enough of it may have survived to provide a dry, good surface for riding from west Norfolk.

---

[80] N.R.O., FC 16/1, op. cit.
[81] For Mary Sewell see p.64.
[82] Curnock, op. cit., vol. iv. p.476.

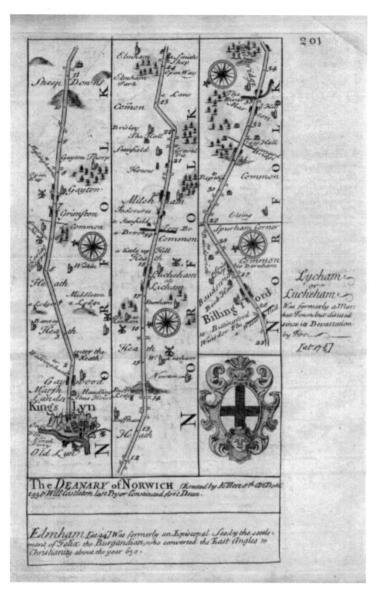

Road map of 1730 of the route between King's Lynn and Billingford. This map, from 'Britannica Depicta,' was published to meet the public demand for a handy-sized road atlas. The maps and engraving are by Emanuel Bowen and the notes are by the antiquarian and lawyer, John Owen.

Botesdale

14 miles north-east of Bury St Edmunds

Tuesday 14 January 1766 – The frozen road being exceeding rough, our machine broke down before day. However, it was patched up so as to carry us to Botesdale.[83]

*   *   *   *   *   *   *

After spending the night at Bury St Edmunds, the coach that Wesley took before dawn the following morning was not robust enough to cope with the poor state of the road. The repairs made to it allowed it to limp into Botesdale. It appears that Wesley made no attempt to preach there. He was faced with a very lengthy journey to Yarmouth and, no doubt, wished to be off as soon as possible.

Bury St Edmunds

23 miles north-east of Ipswich

Tuesday 19 January 1762 – I rode to Bury and was glad to find a little, serious company still. But there cannot be much done here till we preach abroad, or at least in the heart of the town. We are now quite at one end and people will not come from the other till they have first 'tasted the good word.[84]

*   *   *   *   *   *   *

Although it was not recorded in John Wesley's journal, it appears that the Wesley brothers, together with two friends, travelled to the town in July 1754. Charles noted in his diary that the little party, riding on horseback, reached Bury St Edmunds and then rode ten miles further on before stopping for the night. Charles gives no impression of the town on that occasion.

Bury St Edmunds was already the long-established home of various dissenting groups. A Presbyterian chapel had been built in 1690 and was

---

[83] Ibid., vol. v, p.153.
[84] Ibid., vol. iv, p.486.

45

rebuilt in 1711. In addition there were Quaker meeting houses as well as an Independent chapel built in 1716.

The first mention of Bury St Edmunds by John Wesley is when he records that Charles Skelton, one of his itinerant preachers, announced his intention of settling in the town. The fact that he proposed to remain there meant that he had decided to be a Methodist itinerant preacher no longer, for preachers were required to move on to wherever Wesley wished them to be stationed.

Charles Skelton was renowned for his near miraculous conversion of three criminals on their way to the scaffold at Tyburn. That two of the men were Roman Catholics was a cause for even greater celebration and renown for Skelton.[85]

There was no doubt that Skelton was one of those amongst the itinerants who found the control exercised by the Wesleys irksome. In 1751 he asked that Methodist authority should be more widely based and, as John Wesley wrote to his brother, he *pleads for a kind of aristocracy and says you and I should do nothing without the consent* [of] *all the preachers; otherwise we govern arbitrarily to which they cannot submit.* In response to this letter, Charles Wesley narrowed the charge and wrote to John, *You rule the preachers with a rod of iron: they complain of it all over England.*[86]

Clearly the issue of ultimate authority was a thorn in the flesh to some of the early itinerants and a number left Methodism to become independent preachers. Charles Skelton, about whom the Wesleys had asked, *Is his heart with us or is it not?*[87] was one of them. After staying in Bury St Edmunds for a few months, he left the town and became a dissenting minister at a chapel in Southwark.

The entry in John Wesley's journal noting that Skelton was living at Bury St Edmunds was made on 21 April 1754. Perhaps Skelton had begun missionary work in the town, for just four weeks later, the dwelling house and barn of Elizabeth Austin were registered for religious worship for Protestant Dissenters.

John Wesley visited the town again on his second visit to East Anglia in the summer of 1755, saying that he was exhausted. His journal suggests that he did no more than rest there for the night, but his habit was to preach wherever he was and whatever the state of his health and, indeed, his sermon register shows that he preached two sermons in the town.

---

[85] *Arminian Magazine* (later *Methodist Magazine*), 1779, p.92-5. He died in 1798 aged 73.
[86] Charles Wesley ms, 'The Preachers,' 1751.
[87] *Letters of the Rev. John Wesley*, op. cit., vol. iii, p.75.

In 1758, he rode to Bury St Edmunds on his way to Colchester, after spending a week in Norwich. He managed to preach twice to the people gathered there to hear him in spite of feeling very ill.

In bitter weather in January 1761, Wesley made the reverse journey travelling from Colchester to Norwich. He writes that he would like to have stayed on in Bury for a few days because of the severity of the weather, but felt he should press on the next day as -

> *I had work to do elsewhere. So I took horse soon after preaching in the evening...I never before felt so piercing a wind as that which met us in riding out of the gate at daybreak. To think of looking up was a vain thing; I knew not whether I should not lose one of my eyes. The wind affected it as if I had received a severe blow, so that I had no use of it for a time...However, we hobbled on, through miserable roads...*[88]

To make matters worse, they were given inadequate directions and lost their way.

Hostility to the Methodists must have gathered force for when Wesley visited the town in October 1763, he found that mobs were running riot against them. On one evening, with disorder disrupting a service, a stranger from London suddenly stepped forward and taking control of the situation, restored order.

The town was a busy junction for travellers, with several turnpikes converging there. A large number of coaching inns served the travellers and conducted a busy trade. In later life, John Wesley frequently used the coaches from the town to travel to London, Colchester, King's Lynn, Yarmouth and Norwich.

In December 1766, a dwelling house in the Horsemarket (later re-named St Mary's Square) which had been bequeathed by Samuel Manning to his sister, Hannah Jewers, was licensed for Methodist worship.[89] Eventually in 1780, after the death of Hannah Jewers, part of the house was purchased for exclusive use as a Methodist chapel by Richard Cooper, who paid the daughters of Hannah Jewers, Hannah and Elizabeth, ten pounds a year and left them to occupy two other rooms in the building. The rest of the house was known as the 'Methodist Chapel.'

---

[88] Curnock, op. cit., vol. iv, p.431.
[89] The house was demolished in 1811 and a purpose-built chapel was erected on the site. *The Story of Methodism in Bury St Edmunds, 1754-2003*, W.D. Horton, 2003, pp.5-6.

The first Methodist chapel in St Mary's Square.
It was closed in 1878. The doorway was remodelled in the twentieth
century.

By 1769, a small formal Methodist society had been formed. From this time onwards, John Wesley visited the town every year until 1775 when he preached to *the largest congregation I ever saw there.*[90]

Suddenly, there was a cessation of visits and it was not until October 1790 that John Wesley returned to Bury St Edmunds, this time accompanied by his two travelling companions, the preachers Joseph Bradford and Thomas Tattershall. He preached there twice on subsequent evenings *to a deeply attentive congregation.*[91]

It is impossible to know why Wesley left such a long gap between his last two visits. From 1785, the new turnpike road between Colchester and Lowestoft and on to Yarmouth was open so perhaps the improving state of the roads allowed him to travel faster between the places he most needed to visit and he was no longer obliged to break his journey at Bury St Edmunds.

This final visit of John Wesley to the town was reported in the *Bury Post* which recorded the large congregations who attended his preaching at the three services he took there and commented, *The indefatigable labours of*

---

[90] Curnock, op. cit., vol. vi, p.8.
[91] Ibid., vol. viii, p.109.

this venerable old gentleman, now in his 89th year of his age, are truly astonishing.[92]

Caister-on-Sea

3 miles north of Yarmouth

Tuesday 28 November 1786 – About noon, I preached at Caistor [sic], a little town twenty miles east of Norwich to a little serious congregation; the greater part of them seemed to be ripe for a blessing.[93]

*   *   *   *   *   *   *

John Wesley came to Caister by chaise from Norwich. On hearing that Wesley was to preach, one man collected stones and carried them in his pocket ready to pelt the preacher. Instead, he found himself listening with rapt attention and was converted that day.

Two years later, John Wesley visited Caister again, this time in the company of Richard Reece, one of the itinerant preachers stationed in the Norwich circuit. Reece recorded the visit to Caister in his own journal. They dined at Yarmouth and

> *after dinner he walked more than three miles and preached again [at Caister]; with a good deal of pleasure, he walked back to Yarmouth and preached at night with a good deal of vivasity [sic] and life. It is certainly a very singular case for a man more than 86 years of age to go through such fatigues as would overcome most of his preachers of not more than 50.*[94]

A small Methodist society of thirteen members was recorded in 1785 in the circuit book by the itinerant minister. In June 1805, a licence was obtained to hold Methodist meetings in the house of Clement Burton, the man who had originally intended to throw the stones and now an ardent and faithful member of the Methodist congregation in Caister.

---

[92] *Bury Post*, 27 October 1790.
[93] Curnock, vol. vii, p.224.
[94] John Wesley was 85 at this time. N.R.O., FC 17/151, The Journal of Richard Reece.

Copdock

3 miles south-west of Ipswich

Monday 20 January 1766 ... In the evening, the machine put up at the White Elm.[95]

* * * * * * *

After a few days in Norwich in January 1766, Wesley left the city and took the coach for Colchester. The coach stopped for the night at Copdock and the travellers put up at the White Elm Inn. They set out again the following morning and soon afterwards reached Colchester.

Copdock, on the old Roman road and eighteenth-century coach route between Norwich and Colchester, must have seen Wesley pass through on a number of occasions, but John Wesley does not mention the town again until right at the end of his life when on the 13 October 1790, he says that he took the coach from Colchester intending to travel to Norwich. *We set out early*, he wrote, *but found no horses at Copdock; so that we were obliged to go round by Ipswich and wait there half an hour.*[96]

On this journey, John Wesley read Jonathan Carver's *Travels through the Interior Parts of North America in the years 1766, 1767 and 1768.*

Jonathan Carver

[95] Curnock, op. cit., vol. v, p.154.
[96] Ibid., vol. viii, p.105.

Carver, an explorer, had ventured further west than any other English explorer before the American Revolution. He described and mapped the landscape through which he travelled on his extensive journeys mainly through Minnesota, Wisconsin and Mississippi and was the first explorer to mention the great mountain range which was later known as the Rockies.

Carver's book, which was published in 1778, was exceedingly popular and very many copies were sold, but as the profits from the book were so slow in reaching him, he was reduced to poverty. When he died in London in 1780, he was still in extreme want. John Wesley's own visit to America in his early life must have made Carver's book of particular interest to him.

John Wesley was a voracious reader, recording the books he read in his diary and journal. He read whilst riding and during the long hours of coach journeys.

Diss

19 miles south-west of Norwich

Wednesday 20 October 1790 – I had appointed to preach at Diss, a town near Scole. But the difficulty was, where I could preach? The minister was willing I should preach in the church, but feared offending the Bishop who, going up to London, was within a few miles of the town. But a gentleman, asking the Bishop whether he had any objection to it, was answered, "None at all." I think this church is one of the largest in this country. I suppose it has not been so filled these hundred years.[97]

*   *   *   *   *   *   *

Methodism had first come to Diss about 1770 when the itinerant preacher, Thomas Lee, attempted to preach in the street. He received a hostile reception. The town fire engines were used to shower Lee and the crowd which had gathered to hear him with dirty water whilst the church bells were rung with discordant clashes so that his voice could not be heard.

Thomas Lee then moved on to the outskirts of the town, but his renewed attempts to preach were drowned by the shouts of his opponents who rained missiles on him until he abandoned preaching and left Diss altogether.

---

[97] Ibid., vol. vol. viii, pp.108-9.

Watching and listening in the hostile crowd and joining in throwing missiles was George Taylor, a boy of about eight. Soon afterwards, he moved to Bath and in later years was converted there and became an ardent Methodist. His work as a saddler took him to London and then in 1782 he returned to Diss in order to visit his parents.

He was shocked by the sinfulness of the inhabitants. He hired a room and invited the Norwich circuit preachers. As a result, Joshua Keighley decided to visit Diss and preach there. When news of his intention reached the town, soldiers settled themselves in the room before one of the services, filling almost all the seats and began smoking and talking. Keighley then drew from his pocket a copy of the Toleration Act and read it out to them. The soldiers put out their pipes and some crept out of the room whist those who chose to remain, took part in the service and listened to the sermon.

George Taylor's son wrote of other annoyances;

> *At another time, the rioters fastened the door of the house while the congregation were assembled and a person blew in through the keyhole a quantity of asafoetida; the consequence of which would probably have been serious to some, had not Mr Taylor's mother, a woman of resolute and undaunted courage...forced open the door and occupying the doorway, defied the mob to approach. The firmness of her manner imposed awe upon the disturbers and was a means of procuring a circulation of air and consequent relief. Many were greatly affected with the noxious effluvia among whom was the Preacher who was taken to the house of Mr Taylor's mother extremely unwell.*[98]

Other itinerant preachers encountered severe opposition in Diss and after George Taylor had returned to London, the preaching room was closed. When he returned to the town in 1788, another room was hired and the Methodist preachers again supplied the preaching. A class was formed with George Taylor as class leader.

In June 1789, a small chapel was built.[99] The owner of the land had been persuaded to sell to the Methodists by Mrs Hey. She and her husband George were the Governor and Governess of the Diss Workhouse and members of the Methodist society in the town. However, there were relatively few seats in the chapel so that when John Wesley proposed to

---

[98] *Wesleyan Methodist Magazine*, 1826, vol. xliv, pp.64-6.
[99] Diss became head of a separate circuit in 1790.

preach in the town, application was made to the Rector, the Rev. William Manning, by the Methodist Assistant (Superintendent), Thomas Carlill, for the use of the church. The Rector readily agreed and advised Carlill to mention the matter to the Bishop of Norwich, George Horne, who was staying nearby. George Horne and John Wesley had met and talked together on the previous Sunday when Wesley was attending the service in the Cathedral. Now, the Bishop, after enquiring about the time of the service, expressed his own support saying, "Mr Wesley is a brother" and indicated that he would attend.

The church of St Mary the Virgin, Diss

The Bishop and Wesley thought well of each other. The former had written a commentary on the Psalms which John Wesley judged was *the best that ever was wrote.*[100] George Horne, for his part, when asked if Wesley might be allowed to preach at Diss replied that he *would not have Wesley, an ordained minister of the Church of England, forbidden to preach in his diocese.*[101]

John Wesley was detained on his way to Diss and arrived in the town two hours after the time appointed for him to preach. He found the parish church crowded with many from the most respectable families in the

[100] Curnock, op. cit., vol. iv, p.490 fn.
[101] Ibid., vol. viii, p.108 fn.

neighbourhood including several from the family who had given hospitality to the Bishop.

A document giving further details of this visit to Diss was discovered in a safe at Wesley's Chapel in London in 1825. The manuscript tells that the Bishop's host was a Mr Freer who, at the end of the service, came to see John Wesley in the church vestry and asked him about the ordinations he had performed for several of his itinerant preachers. Wesley was about to respond when several of his friends came in and disturbed the conversation, not because they suspected trouble from Mr Freer, but because they were concerned that Wesley should reach Bury St Edmunds in time for his service there.

It appears that a number of people were converted by Wesley's sermon at Diss. In addition, Mr Freer introduced family prayers in his household and a number of his neighbours did the same from that time.

Sarah Mallet of Long Stratton spent some time preaching in and around Diss in 1790. She had written to tell John Wesley about her work there and in one of his last letters, he commended her.[102] Her friend and fellow preacher, Elizabeth Reeve of Redgrave, may well have been converted by Sarah Mallet. Wesley asked Sarah to bring Elizabeth to meet him at Diss so that he might talk to her himself and examine her call to preach. He encouraged the two women in their friendship and support for each other.[103]

Downham Market

40 miles west of Norwich

Tuesday 25 October 1785 – The difficulty was how to get to London. No coach set out till Friday morning nor get in till Saturday night. So I took a post-chaise after preaching and reached Downham between ten and eleven; but here we were informed that, in so dark a night, we could not travel over Ely roads which run between two banks, across which are many bridges where the coachman must drive to an inch; but we knew in whom

---

[102] John Telford, vol. viii, p.250, letter dated 13 Dec. 1790. For Sarah Mallet, see pp.83-4.
[103] Elizabeth Reeve died in 1804. Her obituary was included in the *Methodist Magazine*, but no mention was made of her preaching activities. By this time, the preaching of women was heavily frowned upon by the Wesleyan Conference.

we trusted and pushed forward till about one on Thursday we reached London.[104]

*   *   *   *   *   *   *

John Wesley had been visiting the Methodists in King's Lynn where two of his young preachers had enlivened the spirituality of the society. Anxious to return to London as soon as possible, he tried to make progress by travelling south via Downham Market. He did not leave Lynn until after evening worship so arrived very late at Downham Market. There is no mention of him preaching or meeting any Methodists there. He was obviously keen to press on with his journey.

The road south to Ely was a dangerous one, running alongside the Great Ouse for a large part of its way. Wesley's impatience, as so often happened, overcame all advice for caution and he insisted on continuing his journey without delay. With the skill of the coachman and, Wesley felt, divine help, by half past seven the next morning he was breakfasting at Royston.

Although John Wesley did not mention that there were any Methodists in Downham, a small Methodist congregation was in existence by 1790.

East Dereham

16 miles west-north-west of Norwich

Friday 3 October 1788 - I set out for Norwich in the coach oddly called the 'Expedition.' Going through Dereham about noon, I was desired to preach, which I willingly did...[105]

*   *   *   *   *   *   *

After two days at Lynn where he *spent all the time with much satisfaction*, John Wesley left the town. His coach was not the usual one which ran on the route, for the 'Expedition' was a stage coach which usually travelled between Norwich and London. The regular conveyances between Lynn and Norwich were the 'Lynn and Norwich Diligence' and the 'Lynn Diligence.' The former took eight hours to make the journey via Swaffham and Dereham, starting out from the White Lion in Lynn and

---

[104] Curnock, op. cit., vol. vii, p.122. Comparing the text of Wesley's journal entry with that of his diary, it would appear that the journal was misdated and should have borne the date 'Wednesday 26 October.'
[105] Ibid, op. cit., vol. vii, p.440.

ending at the White Swan in the parish of St Peter Mancroft in Norwich. It arrived in time for any passengers who wished to transfer without delay to the Yarmouth coach and ran every Monday, Wednesday and Friday, returning to Lynn the following day.

The 'Lynn Diligence' made the reverse journey on those days, setting off from the King's Head in Norwich market place and finishing its journey at the Crown Inn in Lynn.

On this journey from Lynn, John read some of his brother Charles' poems in the coach. The stage coach made its first stop at Swaffham where he refreshed himself with tea and where the horses were changed. The coach and its passengers then went on to East Dereham where they found the weekly market in progress in the square.

John Wesley had not intended to preach at Dereham. It is not known who it was that approached him with the request to speak. Had news that he would be passing through the town at that time gone ahead of him or did someone at Dereham recognise the diminutive figure with his white hair and clerical dress?

Although his journal states that he preached from Isaiah, chapter 37, verse 3[106], his diary records that his text on this occasion was John, chapter 17, verse 1,[107] a far less forbidding passage.

In the autumn of 1789, John Wesley again arrived in East Dereham from Lynn by coach. He ate lunch there and at half-past two took a coach, arriving in Norwich in time for tea.

Twelve months later, when the aged Wesley was in Norwich, he proposed to travel to Lynn, but finding that no coach was available in Lynn, he hired a chaise to take him on his journey. In East Dereham, he celebrated communion with the Methodist society. He then tried to procure fresh horses to continue his journey. His search proved unsuccessful and so he was obliged to press on with his tired animals.

---

[106] Isaiah 37 v.3 - *And they said unto him, Thus saith Hezekiah, This day is a day of trouble, and of rebuke, and of blasphemy: for the children are come to the birth and there is not strength to bring forth* – King James Bible.

[107] John 17 v.1 - *These words spake Jesus, and lifted up his eyes to heaven and said' Father, the hour is come; glorify thy Son, that thy Son may also glorify thee'-* King James Bible.

Fakenham

24 miles north-west of Norwich

Monday 29 October 1781 – I went to Fakenham and in the evening preached in the room built by Miss Franklin, now Mrs Parker. I believe most of the town were present.[108]

      *   **

John Wesley does not say why he visited Fakenham. It was not reached by a turnpike road at this time nor was it on a direct route to King's Lynn which was Wesley's destination. However, it seems likely that having promised to visit Wells after John Keed's invitation to visit the Countess of Huntingdon's Connexion meeting there[109] and having heard of Mary Parker's preaching mission in the surrounding villages, he may have wished to pursue this enquiry further and visit the home town of Mary Parker.

At this time, there was a great deal of activity in north Norfolk by the Calvinistic Methodists belonging to the Countess of Huntingdon's Connexion although John Wesley's journal is largely silent about this. One of its preachers, Thomas Mendham of Briston, had built a chapel in his village in 1783 and one of the preachers at the Briston chapel was Elizabeth Grieves, the sister of Mary Parker.[110]

A house in Fakenham belonging to Mary Franklin, spinster, was given a Bishop's licence for religious worship on the 20 July 1773. The building was called the 'New Chapel.'[111] In 1779, Mary Franklin transferred the property to Trustees, one of whom, Thomas Parker, she then married. Soon after, the chapel in Fakenham seems to have been used for a combination of Wesleyan Methodists and the Calvinistic Methodists belonging to the Countess's Connexion. However, as the chapel was by then nominally Wesleyan Methodist, it was incorporated into the King's Lynn Wesleyan Circuit.

In 1782 when stationed in the town, the Assistant of the Lynn circuit, John Prickard, became seriously ill. He was cared for by Thomas and Mary Parker who *'spared no pains or expense in providing everything convenient*

---

[108] Curnock, op. cit., vol. vi, p338.
[109] See p.100.
[110] I am very grateful to Margaret Bird for this information. Thomas Mendham registered a number of premises for religious worship in Norfolk.
[111] NRO, DN DIS 1/2, op. cit.

for me.[112] Whilst Prickard was unable to work, Thomas Carlill, the Assistant in the Colchester Circuit, was sent to Lynn to take his place as a temporary measure. John Wesley wrote to him with advice;

> *....I do not doubt but you will see good days in and about Fakenham, though the people yet do not know much of discipline – and no wonder, if they have never yet had the Rules of our Societies. First explain them at large, and afterwards enforce them, very mildly and very steadily. Molly Franklin and Sister Proudfoot*[113] *are good women. Deal very gently with them, and lovingly labour to convince those whom it concerns of the evil of buying or selling on the Lord's Day.*[114]

Early in 1784, Mary Parker wrote to John Wesley. She told him that the Methodist society in Fakenham was harmonious and growing in numbers and spirituality. However, she indicated that issues remained and that all was not completely well. It appears that some people had left the society, but had promised to return if Wesley's preachers stopped preaching there. They complained that the doctrine of 'perfection' was preached and that *while one of them was preaching, several persons were suddenly and violently affected.*

Mary Parker's chapel

---

[112] *The Early Methodist Preachers*, Thomas Jackson, 1866, London, vol. iv, p.193.

[113] Mary Proudfoot was another of the women who missioned the area around Fakenham.

[114] *Letters*, Telford, op. cit., vol. vii, pp.116-17.

Wesley's reply dealt with these issues reported by Mary Parker. He felt that she *ought never to have joined with or received persons of such a spirit. What a narrow popish spirit was this! What vile bigotry!* He challenged her about preaching perfection and pointed out that perfection was *loving God with all our heart* and achieving a sense of communion with God. It was a state sought by Methodists and, from what they said and wrote, a goodly number appear to have reached such a plane of perfection.

As for the second complaint, he asked if she had read his journals and other accounts of conversion which showed that such signs were evidence of an inward transformation. Although such violent emotionalism was not actively encouraged by Wesley, some people were overcome during services and fell to the ground, wept or showed other signs of agitation.

Finally, he felt these were poor reasons to advance for stopping the Methodist preachers supplying the Fakenham pulpit and wrote that those who wish to do so *are maintaining a bad cause.*[115] Presumably those who left the preaching house cared neither for the doctrine of perfection nor the behaviour of some members of the congregation.

Some time after the death of Mary Parker and her husband and children in 1788, the congregation divided permanently. The Calvinists moved to another meeting place leaving the chapel entirely in Methodist hands.

Felsham

8 miles south-east of Bury St Edmunds

Tuesday 5 November 1771 - ...We called at Felsham, near which is the seat of the late Mr Reynolds. The house is, I think, the best contrived and the most beautiful I ever saw. It has four fronts, and five rooms on a floor, elegantly, though not sumptuously, furnished. At a small distance stands a delightful grove. On every side of this, the poor rich man, who had no hope beyond the grave, placed seats, to enjoy life as long as he could. But being resolved none of his family should be 'put into the ground,' he built a structure in the midst of the grove, vaulted above and beneath, with niches for coffins, strong enough to stand for ages. In one of these he had soon the satisfaction of laying the remains of his only child; and, two years after, those of his wife. After two years more, in the year 1759, having eat and

---

[115] Ibid., vol. vii, pp.205-7.

drank and forgotten God for eighty-four years, he went himself to give an account of his stewardship.[116]

*   *   *   *   *   *   *

John Reynolds was a High Sheriff of Suffolk in 1735. Local tradition tells that he quarrelled bitterly with the vicar of Felsham. As a result of the feud, Reynolds vowed never again to enter the parish church and determined that under no circumstances would his own or his family's remains be buried in the churchyard.

The mausoleum was built in yellow brick with red brick decoration and the square structure was ornamented with blank windows. It remains, now totally ruinous, far off in a field behind the house, which is now known as Mausoleum House.

Forncett End

8 miles north-east of Diss

Sunday 25 March 1759 – I rode to Forncett, twelve miles from Norwich where also was a building of James Wheatley's which without my desire he had included in the lease. We found William Cudworth had preached there in the morning....The people looked as direful upon me as if I had been Satan in person. However, they flocked from all parts, so that the Tabernacle would not near contain them. I preached about two; God bare witness to his truth and many were cut to the heart. After preaching I found Mr Cudworth sitting in the pulpit behind me, whom I quietly and silently passed by.

Wednesday 28 March 1759 – I rode over to Forncett again and preached to a large congregation. [A] great part of them were now exceedingly softened, but some were still bitter as wormwood.[117]

*   *   *   *   *   *   *

At Forncett End, a meeting house called 'The Tabernacle' had been built in the late autumn of 1754 by the followers of James Wheatley. When John

---

[116] Curnock, op. cit., vol. v, p.435.
[117] Ibid., vol. iv, pp.303-4.

Wesley took over the lease of the Norwich Tabernacle in 1759, this building was also included in the contract.

William Cudworth ministered to several congregations of his own in London before coming to Norwich to assist James Wheatley. He often took services in the Tabernacles in Norwich and Forncett and continued to preach after Wheatley's disgrace. His Calvinistic stance brought him into sharp conflict with John Wesley who adopted an unremitting opposition to him. The two men disliked each other intensely; Wesley wrote that Cudworth and his supporters abhorred him *as much as they do the pope and ten times more than they do the devil.*[118] Cudworth, for his part, was accustomed to go into the pulpit after John Wesley had finished preaching and criticize and condemn the sermon. Perhaps Cudworth in his morning address had disparaged Wesley and that explained the hostile response and black looks of many in the very crowded congregation on this visit by John Wesley to Forncett End.

The Tabernacle at Forncett End

Two days later, Wesley interviewed William Cudworth. As a result, he concluded that Cudworth's opinions were uniquely his own and entirely new; that Cudworth believed that those who differed from these views

[118] *Life and Times of the Rev. John Wesley, MA*, Luke Tyerman, 1890, London, vol. ii, pp.400-1.

worship another God; and that he is incapable as a brute beast of being convinced even in the smallest point.[119] John Wesley was not alone in being unable to get along with Cudworth. George Whitefield, too, had problems and found him impossible to work with. Eventually Cudworth moved back to London and set up his own church there.

When John Wesley visited Forncett End again the following year, he found the congregation to be *a much milder people than I left there.*[120]

After John Wesley gave up the lease of the Norwich Tabernacle, he also relinquished the Tabernacle at Forncett. The building was then bought by the Countess of Huntingdon for her Connexion for £900. Seven trustees were appointed to oversee secular matters. In addition, they were given the power to appoint or dismiss ministers there as they thought fit. Eventually the building was taken over by the Baptists.

Built of clay lump, it was bricked round and a porch was also added by the Baptist congregation in 1875 as a testimonial to their preacher, George Maddeys, on his twentieth anniversary as a minister there.

In the middle of the twentieth century, the chapel closed and became a farm store. It is now almost derelict and in the last year, the few gravestones which survived at the front of the chapel have disappeared.

Haddiscoe

7 miles north-west of Lowestoft

Wednesday 27 October 1784 – 9 chaise; 12 Haddiscoe; dinner; Hebrews 7, 25; chaise.[121]

*   *   *   *   *   *   *

This brief entry in John Wesley's diary hides a great deal of activity.

In his old age, William Lorkin, who was a member of Cherry Lane Methodist chapel in Norwich, wrote a history of the early years of Methodism in the city.[122] He recorded that at this time, the Norwich

---

[119] Curnock, op. cit., vol. iv, p.303.
[120] Ibid., p.363.
[121] Ibid., vol. vii, p.28.
[122] *A Concise History of the First Establishment of Wesleyan Methodist in the City of Norwich*, William Lorkin, Norwich, 1825.

congregation was greatly troubled by Sandemanian opponents[123] who were continually attempting to sow discord and confusion. In consequence, one of Wesley's preachers, Charles Atmore, came to Norwich to help deal with this difficult situation. Atmore was a Norfolk man who had been born at Heacham. His mother had died when he was eighteen months old and as his father, a sea captain, was away at sea for long periods, Charles was brought up by his aunt and uncle at Haddiscoe.

He was introduced to John Wesley in February 1781 during one of Wesley's visits to Norwich. Wesley then appointed him to work as an additional preacher in the Norwich Circuit and thereafter he became a full-time itinerant preacher. He was then appointed to the Grimsby Circuit, but contracted the 'ague' and he returned to Haddiscoe to recover from this malarial illness and convalesce at the home of his relatives. While he was there, John Wesley sent him a recommendation to take 'Dr Sander's pills.' The pills consisted of Castile soap and arsenic. Wesley assured Charles Atmore that the prescription *seldom fails.* [124]

Charles Atmore, itinerant preacher and one of John Wesley's closest colleagues. He published an account of the lives of the early Methodist preachers and also a description of the beginnings of Methodism in the United States.

---

[123] Sandemanians (or Glasites) belonged to a small sect which originated in Scotland in the 1730s. They had a number of unusual rites such as washing each other's feet. They believed amongst other things that faith was sufficient and it did not need to be demonstrated in a good life or in good works.

[124] *Letters*, ed. Telford, op. cit., vol. vii, p.124.

After John Wesley had preached in Norwich on Wednesday 27 October 1784, he and Charles Atmore travelled by chaise to Haddiscoe, the home of Atmore's uncle and aunt, William and Mary Lamb. Atmore wrote in his journal, *We were honoured with his company at Haddiscoe to dine. He afterwards preached a short but sweet sermon from Hebrews 7, 25.*[125]

On leaving Haddiscoe, Wesley travelled on to Yarmouth. For the first couple of miles of the journey, he travelled across the wetland by a winding raised causeway constructed in mediaeval times to provide a safe route across the Waveney marshes.

An entry in the Norwich circuit book written eight months after John Wesley's visit to the village lists fourteen members of the Wesleyan society. William Lamb, farmer, was the class leader.

Around the year 1779, William Lamb had heard the Methodist preacher, Mary Sewell, speak in a little house at the nearby village of Thurlton and was greatly moved by her sermon. She was listed in the circuit book in 1785 as a local preacher, so it appears that she had been formally recognised by the itinerant ministers. However, there was great disquiet and some hostility to women preachers from many Methodist preachers, yet John Wesley himself was convinced of Mary's call to preach.

Mary Sewell spoke in a number of Norwich towns and villages. Adam Clarke, one of the most prominent of Wesley's ministers, visited the Norwich circuit in 1784 and also heard her preach. He was so impressed that he declared his hostility to women preachers was altered; *this woman's preaching has done much good; and fruits of it may be found copiously in different places in the circuit.*[126]

The parish church of St Mary stands on an eminence high above the surrounding marshes. In the churchyard close to the church is an impressive dark stone tombstone. Its lettering is deeply cut and it has withstood the weathering. The inscription reads –

This stone was
erected by the Revd
CHARLES ATMORE as a Monument of filial Affection
to the MEMORY of
WILLIAM and MARY LAMB

---

[125] 'The Journal of Charles Atmore', *Wesleyan Methodist Magazine*, 1845, no. 68, pp.15-16. *Wherefore he is able also to save them to the uttermost that came unto God by him, seeing he ever liveth to make intercession for them.* King James Bible.
[126] 'Journal of Adam Clarke', quoted in *An Account of the Life of Adam Clarke*, ed. J.B.B. Clarke, 1833, London, vol. i, pp.215-16.

who lived together in Conjugal Affection
for sixty-two years and in their death they were not (long) divided.
She died Jany 13th 1813; Aged 92 Years.
He died March 17th 1815 in the 90th Year of his Age.

'Blessed are the dead who die in the Lord.'

St Mary's Church, Haddiscoe
The tombstone of William and
Mary Lamb is just beyond the round tower.

Haverhill

17 miles south-west of Bury St Edmunds

Tuesday 5 January 1762 – As we rode through Haverhill, we were saluted
with one huzza, the mob of that town having no kindness for Methodists.

Wednesday 6 January 1762 – In the afternoon it blew a storm, by the favour of which we came into Haverhill quite unmolested. But, notwithstanding wind and rain, the people crowded so fast into the preaching-house that I judged it best to begin half an hour before the time, by which means it contained the greater part of them. Although they that could not come in made a little noise, it was a solemn and an happy season.

Thursday 7 January 1762 – Abundance of them came again at five and drank in every word. Here also, many followed me into the house and hardly knew how to part. At nine I preached.[127]

        *   *   *   *   *   *   *

John Wesley travelled to this part of Suffolk after a visit to Everton in Bedfordshire, riding through Cambridgeshire. Although his arrival in Haverhill was greeted by shouts from the mob, no physical violence occurred. He did not stop in the town, but went on to the small village of Stoke-by-Clare about five miles away, returning to Haverhill the following day.

In Haverhill, a dwelling house and barn belonging to John Adams had been licensed for religious worship on the 21 April 1761. It is likely, therefore, that Wesley used the barn for preaching to the large numbers who had heard of his visit.

Although the Quakers, Presbyterians and Baptists had long been established in Haverhill, the authorities were obviously hostile to any Methodist activity in the town. In January 1761, a year before John Wesley's visit, it was

> *ordered that the Churchwardens and Overseers do go to the owner or occupier of the houses, barns or other places where the itinerant teachers hold forth and demand of them a proper licence for the place or places they do hold forth in, and if no licence is produced, then the said Churchwardens and Overseers shall indict them at the next quarter sessions to be held at Bury and the next general quarter sessions to be held at Colchester as a common nuisance.*[128]

---

[127] Curnock, op. cit., vol. iv, pp.483-4.
[128] Haverhill Parish Book, 5 January 1761; quoted in *A History of Congregationalism in Norfolk and Suffolk*, John Browne, 1877, London, pp.190-1.

It appears, therefore, that there had been some Methodist preaching in Haverhill from itinerant preachers and that this had come to the attention of the town authorities. Certainly it was necessary to obtain a licence to use a building for religious worship before meetings could be held there and such a licence had to be obtained from the bishop. If meetings for worship were being held in an unlicensed building, then the law was being flouted and if it was John Adams who was allowing his house and barn to be used in this way, then he was somewhat tardy in applying for a licence; it was another three-and-a-half months after the churchwardens were stirred into action before the necessary document was applied for and obtained.

Despite John Wesley's visit, no further mention is made of the town in his journal and no formal Methodist society was formed there. It was many years before Methodist activity was once more seen in the town.

Hempnall

9 miles south of Norwich

Tuesday 4 September 1759 – I walked to Kemnall[129]...and preached at one o'clock. The ringleader of the mob came with his horn, as usual, before I began. But one quickly catched and threw away his horn, and in a few minutes he was deserted by all his companions who were seriously and deeply attentive to the great truth, 'By grace ye are saved through faith.[130]

*   *   *   *   *   *   *

On 15 January 1754, an application was made to the Bishop of Norwich by James Wheatley, William Robarts, Samuel and John Baldwin, William Bailey, Matthew Tuck and John Fuller for a licence to register the dwelling house of William Robarts and John Fuller in Hempnall for religious worship. The certificate was duly given and meetings for worship were begun there under the oversight of James Wheatley.[131]

It would appear that since John Wesley had taken over the lease of the Tabernacle in Norwich the previous December, he was also concerned for the other two congregations supervised by Wheatley – at Forncett End

---

[129] A mis-spelling by Wesley.
[130] *Ephesians* 2, v.8; Curnock, op. cit., vol. iv, p.351.
[131] N.R.O., DN DIS 1/2, op. cit.

which he had visited on his last expedition to Norfolk in April 1759 and then this congregation at Hempnall which he inspected later in the year.

Perhaps the congregation had lost its home for local tradition states that on his only visit to Hempnall, John Wesley preached under an oak tree growing on a small piece of grass at the bottom of The Street. This oak tree was cut down in the twentieth century to make way for the village war memorial.[132]

In his sermon register, Wesley entered two texts for this visit to Hempnall. It suggests that he preached here not only at lunch time, but again later in the day. He then walked the nine miles back to Norwich.

There is a local story about Samuel Head, a higgler[133] and innkeeper, who happened to be travelling through Hempnall on the day that John Wesley was preaching there. Seeing people flocking to listen to Wesley, Head decided to hear him, too. He was so impressed by what he heard, that he resolved to give up his dishonest ways and he turned his disorderly inn at Wicklewood into a Methodist preaching house.

Adam Clarke, one of the Methodist itinerant preachers stationed in the Norwich circuit in 1783, claimed later that at this time, Hempnall was one of the places regularly visited by the preachers. However, no Methodist society at Hempnall was mentioned in the earliest surviving lists of societies and members in 1785, 1786, 1787.

Herringswell

9½ miles north-west of Bury St Edmunds

Wednesday 18 March 1767 – I preached at Herringswell and the next day came to Norwich.[134]

*   *   *   *   *   *   *

Wesley had spent the previous day in Colchester and then had travelled north through Suffolk. There is no indication as to why he should have left the turnpike road to preach at the small village of Herringswell.

---

[132] The Rev. C.A. Walker, then of Attleborough, wrote 'when there some time ago, I heard references made to Wesley's visit, and a tree in the centre of the village is still spoken of as Wesley's tree.' *Proceedings of the Wesley Historical Society*, vol. iv. However, this was written more than 140 years after John Wesley's visit to Hempnall.

[133] A higgler is someone who drives a small cart.

[134] Curnock, op. cit., vol. v, p.196.

It does not appear that he ever called there again. A small Methodist society was in existence in Herringswell from 1790.

Ipswich

Wednesday 13 October 1790 – We were obliged to go round by Ipswich and wait there half an hour.[135]

      *   *   *   *   *   *   *

John Wesley and his companions had set out at half-past four that morning from Colchester, intending to travel to Norwich. A change of horses was planned at Copdock, but none was available and so the travellers were forced to go to Ipswich to try and find fresh horses there.

After a brief wait, they set out again, leaving Ipswich at half-past seven and arrived without further mishap in Norwich early in the afternoon.

On the journey, Wesley passed the time reading Captain Jonathan Carver's book, *Travels Through the Interior Parts of North America,* which he much enjoyed, although he very much regretted the massacre of English people by the native Americans in 1757.[136]

This single brief unplanned stop in Ipswich took place right at the end of John Wesley's life. Methodism did not begin in the town until 1804-5.[137]

It is perhaps puzzling why Wesley ignored Ipswich on his East Anglian visits and made no attempt to preach there. Ipswich, as the county town, might have expected John Wesley's attention especially as he passed close by on many occasions.

Suffolk had provided a fertile soil for Calvinism and consequently, right to the end of the nineteenth century, Methodists faced an uphill struggle in towns and villages from the many Calvinists already established there. By the mid eighteenth century, congregations of Independents, Baptists and Presbyterians were represented in Ipswich as well as Unitarians and Quakers. Perhaps Wesley felt that his time could better be spent where his preaching might fall on more receptive soil. However, he was never slow to face Calvinist opponents elsewhere so his failure to spend time in Ipswich is hard to explain.

---

[135] Ibid., vol. viii, p.105.
[136] See pp..50-1.
[137] *The Story of a Century: the History of Wesleyan Methodism in the Ipswich circuit,* T. Nicholson Ritson, n/d., p.76.

Kenninghall

6 miles north-west of Diss

Friday 4 January 1760 – I preached....in the evening at Kenninghall where the Antinomians had laboured hard in the devil's service. Yet all are not lost; a few are still left 'who walk not after the flesh, but after the Spirit.[138]

*　　*　　*　　*　　*　　*　　*

John Wesley's journal records that he preached three times at Kenninghall – first on Monday 6 November 1758 and again, shortly afterwards on 26 December of the same year. On both these occasions, he spent only a few hours in the village after leaving Norwich and he makes no other comment other than that he preached a sermon on each occasion.

His third visit was on Friday 4 January 1760 when, after leaving Norwich, he rode to Forncett St Peter where he preached at one o'clock. He then went on to Kenninghall. Clearly he found the situation there had deteriorated as a result of heretical activity and that many of his former followers had been seduced by Antinomianism.

Wesley had endless trouble with Antinomians in Norfolk and was to continue to do so in the future. This ancient heresy had raised its head many times down the centuries. Its tenet was that Christians are freed by God's grace from the need to observe any moral law. Hence, any behaviour, however immoral, is blameless. Wesley refuted it again and again, but, in spite of doing so, continued to have persistent trouble with some of his congregations over whom it exerted a great attraction. It particularly appealed to the congregation at the Tabernacle in Norwich where it had been introduced by James Wheatley in 1751.

After leaving Kenninghall, John Wesley rode on to Colchester.

King's Lynn

40 miles north-west of Norwich

Thursday 7 November 1771 – Lynn seems to be considerably larger than Yarmouth; I believe it stands on double the ground and the houses in general are better built – some of them are little palaces. The market-place is a spacious and noble square, more beautiful than either that at Yarmouth

---

[138] Curnock, op. cit., vol. iv, p.363; *Romans*, 8, v. 1, King James Bible.

or Norwich; and the people are quite of another turn, affable and humane. They have the openness and frankness common throughout the county; and they add to it good nature and courtesy... I was desired by the prisoners to give them a word of exhortation. They received it with the utmost eagerness. Who knows but one or two may retain it?[139]

* * * * * * *

John Wesley wrote this account of King's Lynn on his first sight of the town. He visited Lynn on eleven more occasions, usually at two yearly intervals.

Wesley obviously found King's Lynn an attractive town. Daniel Defoe had also written enthusiastically about Lynn after his visit some years before that of John Wesley. *Here are more gentry and consequently is more gaiety in this town than in Yarmouth or even in Norwich itself; the place abounding in very good company.*[140]

The Tuesday Market Place was a spacious open area lined with what William White described as *large and handsome houses, two good inns and several retail shops.*[141] In the centre stood a large stone market cross surrounded by columns which supported an octagonal upper room. Statues in classical style ornamented four sides whilst an open gallery surrounded the building which was surmounted by a dome.

It appears that Methodism in Lynn had first been organised from Norwich. One of the Wesleyan itinerant preachers, George Shadford was sent by John Wesley to supervise the Methodist work in Norwich in 1770. During the course of the year, Shadford said that he went to Lynn occasionally, staying there two or three weeks at a time. His work in Lynn proved to be successful and he formed an organised Methodist society of thirty members.

John Wesley first arrived in the town in November 1771, travelling from Bury St Edmunds in heavy rain. Soon after his arrival, he heard news of a former acquaintance, Betty Fairbridge of Whitby, who had recently settled in Lynn. Once a staunch believer, her faith had flagged. Wesley had met her the previous year and from that time, although seriously ill with

---

[139] Ibid., vol. v, p.436.
[140] *A Tour through the Whole Island of Great Britain*, Daniel Defoe, ed. Pat Rogers, Penguin English Library, 1971, p.97.
[141] William White, *Directory of Norfolk*, 1845, Sheffield, p.522.

71

tuberculosis, she had regained her faith *till prayer was swallowed up in praise* and she died *with triumphant joy*.[142]

During this first visit, Wesley attended the prison at the request of the prisoners, addressing them in both the morning and evening. He also preached twice in the house of John and Mary Crawford[143] in Black Boy Street.[144] The Crawfords had been converted by Wesley and had come to Lynn from the Methodist society in Newcastle-upon-Tyne. They asked John Wesley to send itinerant preachers to Lynn and offered them lodgings and hospitality in their home despite their own poverty. Perhaps this accounts for Wesley's interest in the town and his decision to pay a visit. On this occasion, the house proved too small for all those who wished to hear John Wesley. It was on this same site of the Crawford's house that Tower Street Wesleyan church was built in 1813.

When John Wesley next visited Lynn in November 1773, he found the society in disarray, having been torn apart by Calvinism. He made great efforts to bring about a reconciliation amongst the members, leaving the congregation settled and peaceful.

At the beginning of 1775, Wesley says he preached in the newly-built preaching house in New Conduit Street. The congregation was so large that only about half of those who had gathered to hear him could squeeze into the building. He visited the sick, the members of the Methodist society and those who had fallen away. The following year, the Lynn circuit was created.

On this occasion, John Wesley had with him a difficult companion. One of the London Methodists, Thomas Marriott, a baker, had journeyed to Yarmouth with Wesley and had been taken ill there. Wesley thought him mentally disturbed and offered to send him back to London in his own chaise. Marriott refused the offer and insisted on continuing on with Wesley. Good lodgings had been provided in Norwich for the pair and all seemed well while they were there, but once they arrived in Lynn, Marriott's illness returned. Wesley described him being *ill in body and in a violent agony of mind ... fully believed he was on the point of death, nor could any arguments convince him of the contrary*.[145] On leaving Lynn, Wesley found it *heavy work to get him forward*[146], but they finally reached London safely two days later.

---

[142] Curnock, op. cit., vol. v, p.436.
[143] Mary Crawford was still alive in 1817 aged 103.
[144] Black Boy Street was later renamed Tower Street.
[145] Curnock, op. cit., vol. vi, p.87.
[146] Ibid.

John Wesley found that his visit to Lynn in the autumn of 1785 was a surprise. He said that he had long felt it to be *a cold, comfortless place,*[147] but now he found that a transformation had taken place – *two young, zealous, active preachers....have enlivened both the society and the congregation.*[148]

The following autumn, John Wesley again visited the town, this time travelling on from Cambridge. He said that he had promised to preach in the new preaching house and *I thought it best to go while the good weather continued.*[149] He had intended to arrive in the town at noon on Tuesday 10 October 1786, but the messenger he sent to book the coach, ignored or misunderstood Wesley's instructions and took a seat for him in a later coach which meant Wesley arrived in the town late in the evening and, to his irritation, had less time there than he had intended. This new chapel was situated in North Clough Lane.[150] It was described by a member of the congregation as *very well contrived and neatly fitted up. It is about forty-two feet by thirty feet with very deep galleries in front and at both ends. It is so constructed as to be capable of accommodating perhaps a greater number of hearers than any of our other chapels.*[151]

At the beginning of October 1788, Wesley spent three days in Lynn, staying at the home of John Keed, a friend he had made some years earlier.[152]

In October 1789, he set out from London at 9 pm, travelled overnight and arrived at Barton Mills the following morning. After breakfast, he took a chaise, reaching Lynn at 11.30 am. The weather was dismal and Wesley recorded in his journal that, at the evening service, *the heavy rain prevented tender people from attending in the evening.*[153]

John Wesley's final journey to the town in October 1790 was frustrating. There were no coaches from Norwich on the day he wished to travel and he was forced to go by post-chaise instead. With no change of horses available at Dereham or Swaffham, he found he could only travel on by single-horse

---

[147] Ibid., vol. vii, p.122.
[148] Ibid. It is not clear whether Wesley meant the preachers stationed in Lynn during the previous Connexional year, John Barber and John McKersey or those who were appointed to the circuit for the new year, starting in September, William Palmer and Charles Bland, the latter having just been admitted on trial.
[149] Curnock, op. cit., vol. vii, pp.213-14.
[150] This chapel became too small for the congregation and was replaced by the Tower Street Chapel in 1813. The vacant building was used as a National School for girls.
[151] *The History of Lynn*, William Richards, 1812, King's Lynn, p.1110.
[152] For John Keed and his previous contact with Wesley, see pp.73, 100.
[153] Curnock, op. cit., vol. viii, p.18.

chaise. His vexation was further increased by the wind and rain which blew in their faces throughout the whole journey *so that I was thoroughly chilled from head to foot before I came to Lynn.*[154] It was a most unpleasant journey and must have been very tiring for an old man.

Whilst in Lynn, John Wesley lodged with one of the clergy of St Margaret's, Edward Edwards, at Tower House in Tower Place. It was during this visit that he opened the new chapel in Tower Street. The North Clough Lane building had become far too small as a result of *the late increase in Methodism here.* The replacement chapel which stood on the site of an old Jewish synagogue was *a new and very capacious as well as elegant and splendid place.*[155] Because of the press of people wanting to attend services, immediately it had been lengthened and had had galleries built on three sides.

> *In the evening, all the clergymen in the town, except one who was lame, were present at the preaching. They are all prejudiced in favour of the Methodists; as indeed are most of the townsmen, who give a fair proof by contributing so much to our Sunday schools, so that there is near twenty pounds in hand.*[156]

Such enthusiastic acceptance of John Wesley and the Methodists showed just how far opinion had shifted during the decades of Wesley's work. He left the town for Diss on Wednesday 20 October, sharing a chaise with Thomas Tattershall, one of the itinerant preachers stationed in the Lynn circuit, and Joseph Bradford.

Lakenham

1½ miles south of Norwich

Thursday 11 July 1754 - ...Several came to us [at Lakenham], *entreating us to preach; and at night a great number were gathered together to hear us...*[157]

---

[154] Ibid., vol. viii, p.107.
[155] Richards, op. cit., p.1111.
[156] Curnock, op. cit., vol. viii, p.108.
[157] *Life.* Jackson, op. cit., vol. ii, p.46.

Wednesday 17 July 1754 – In the morning, James Wheatley overtook me and Charles Perronet in our way to Lakenham. I would hope he intended to pass us by; but Charles [Perronet], looking back and spying him, forced him to stop and speak to us. He asked me how I did; to which I made no answer. Charles cried out, "Ride on, James; ride on; do not talk to us. I pray God give you repentance." He asked me then how my brother did; but still I said nothing. Then, recovering himself, he said, "And God give you repentance, Mr Perronet." I bade Charles turn back and leave him; which he did; being grieved at the hardness of his heart.[158]

*　　*　　*　　*　　*　　*　　*

In the middle of the eighteenth century, Lakenham was quite separate from Norwich and the small village extended south as far as Harford Bridges on the River Yare. Its beautiful rural setting by the river made it popular for day excursions from the city. The road to Norwich was a very steep one until it was levelled in 1804 by a cutting through the hillside.

The ancient parish church of St John and All Saints stood on a hill above the village houses. During the eighteenth century it was a notorious haunt of grave robbers.

A list of the inhabitants of the city and surrounding parishes made in 1752, recorded thirty-five houses in Lakenham with a population of 165.

John and Charles Wesley's host was Captain Bartholomew Gallatin of the First Dragoon Guards and his wife. John Wesley had met the couple when they were living in York where the Captain was stationed with his regiment. The Gallatins had subsequently moved to Lakenham and on hearing that the little party consisting of the Wesley brothers, Robert Windsor[159] and Charles Perronet were to visit Norwich, offered them the hospitality of their home. It is not known exactly where the Gallatin's house stood, but Charles Wesley described it as being a mile and a half from Norwich, so it seems likely that it was located in the old village.[160]

The Wesleys had prepared for this visit by sending a letter to the *Norwich Mercury* newspaper at the end of the previous year. In it, they dissociated themselves from James Wheatley and his followers. It proved

---

[158] Ibid., p.48.
[159] John Wesley preached the funeral sermon for Robert Windsor on 7 February 1790. He described him as 'a burning and shining light. He was born a few months after me, was a prudent, serious, diligent man, full of mercy and good fruits, without partiality, and without hypocrisy.' Curnock, op. cit., vol. viii, pp.40-1.
[160] In later years, Lakenham grew until it reached the Norwich city gates.

to be a wise move for, as soon as the Wesley brothers arrived at Lakenham, they heard that the whole city of Norwich was in an uproar in protest at James Wheatley's adulterous behaviour. It was just at this time that the *Norwich Mercury* was filled with accusations, denials and counter accusations from those involved in Wheatley's scandalous sexual indiscretions. A series of pamphlets was also being published stating the positions of the various players. Charles Wesley noted in his journal that the streets were ringing with the news of Wheatley's immoral behaviour.

Captain Gallatin had recently dined with the mayor, John Gay, who had expressed concern at the disorder in the city. In consequence, the little party remained quietly at Lakenham for a few days until the worst of the tumult should die down. Nevertheless, Charles said that he was ready to preach to those people who cared to come to Lakenham to hear him and it was at Lakenham that the first Norfolk Methodist sermon was heard. On subsequent days, Charles again preached to the neighbours at Lakenham. He also prayed with them and engaged them in conversation. He then turned his attention to Norwich.

The news that the Wesley brothers and their Methodist friends had arrived at Lakenham and that Charles had begun preaching in the street in Norwich must have quickly come to the ears of James Wheatley. However, in view of their discovery of his previous immoral behaviour and the current accusations against him, it is odd that James Wheatley felt he could approach Charles Wesley and Charles Perronet in the street. It is not clear what his purpose was.

What exactly did Wheatley's wish that Peronnet would repent mean? There is some suggestion that Perronet, although not an ordained priest in the Anglican church and despite signing an agreement to act in accord with the other preachers, may have administered communion to two of the preachers and to a little congregation in London. Perhaps this was preying on his conscience. At this time, his independent action was unknown to the Wesleys, but Charles, learning of it soon after he had left Norwich, was furiously angry with Perronet. By now, Charles Peronnet, although only thirty-one, was in poor health and had recently made his will. Unable to continue as an itinerant preacher, he was employed by John Wesley to help in publishing *Explanatory Notes upon the New Testament* on which the Wesley brothers were working in the summer of 1754 and which was published the following year.

Mrs Gallatin invited Charles Wesley's wife to join them at Lakenham. Both women attended Charles' early morning preaching on several occasions. Once, the hostile crowd closed in and jostled the stately Mrs Gallatin whom, they assumed, must be the preacher's wife and ignored the little figure of Mrs Sally Wesley.

In comparison with the violence and turbulence he found in the city, Charles appreciated the quiet atmosphere of the house at Lakenham. He wrote of one day, *I enjoyed my long-sought solitude all day at Lakenham*.[161] John spent most of his stay resting at the house and recovering from his illness, although he was well enough to go into Norwich on the Sunday after their arrival and, after Charles had preached, said a few words to the crowd. After ten days at Lakenham, John returned to London whilst Charles stayed on with the Gallatins until the middle of August.

John Gay, Mayor of Norwich, 1754

Artist - Thomas Bardwell (1707-67)

Shortly afterwards, the Gallatins were sent to Canterbury with the regiment. They must have remained in close touch with events in Norwich for they wrote to George Whitefield to urge him to conduct the re-opening services at the Tabernacle after Wheatley's disgrace. Whitefield did conduct the service in August 1755. However, John Wesley regarded this as an unfriendly move and rebuked him for aiding a rival chapel to his own

---

[161] *Life*, Jackson, op. cit., p.52.

in Norwich. Whitefield replied that he had come to Norwich purely to advance the glory of God and that his time was too precious to waste in vindicating himself against those informers who wished to make trouble. John Wesley well knew that the Gallatins had long been friends with George Whitefield and the Countess of Huntingdon, just as he and his brother had been. Nevertheless, in spite of this upset, the Wesleys remained on good terms with the Gallatins and both brothers stayed with them in Canterbury and later in London and at Ham in Surrey where the Gallatins had a country house.

Lakenheath

10 miles west of Thetford and 37 miles south-west of Norwich

Thursday 24 November 1757 – A man had spoken to me the last week as I was going through Thetford and desired me to preach at Lakenheath near Mildenhall in Suffolk. I was purposed so to do and rode thither from Thetford. One, Mr E[vans], had lately built a large and convenient preaching-house there at his own expense. It was more than filled at six o'clock, many standing at the door. At five in the morning (as uncommon a thing as this was in those parts), the house was nearly filled again with earnest, loving, simple people. Several of them came into Mr E's house afterward, stood awhile, and then burst into tears. I promised to call upon them again and left them much comforted.[162]

*   *   *   *   *   *

Clearly a good start had been made. The following year, Wesley was again at Lakenheath where he rested for a day before setting out on a very hard day's ride to Bedford. Six weeks later, he was back at Lakenheath where he preached three sermons. He wrote in his journal a snapshot of the progress of religion in this village. He described how *forty years ago, a poor man lived here who walked with God and was the means of awakening a few others. When these were nearly extinct, Charles Skelton came, awakened a few more, and forsook them.*[163]

---

[162] Curnock, op. cit., vol. iv, pp.244-5.
[163] Ibid., vol. iv, p.297.

Charles Skelton, an actor, became one of Wesley's itinerant ministers in 1749. Even before his commitment to the itinerancy, he was celebrated for converting two condemned Roman Catholic criminals on their journey to the scaffold. His work with Wesley did not last long, however, for soon after, he gave up his Methodist work and settled in Bury St Edmunds.[164] It must have been while he was living there that he visited Lakenheath and held some religious gatherings. Then in 1753, he established himself as an Independent minister in Southwark.

In February 1756, John Evans applied for a religious licence for his house in The Street in Lakenheath and eighteen months later obtained a licence for the chapel which he had built.

Wesley mentioned the congregation to his friend, the Anglican Rev. Martin Madan,[165] a firm friend then based at Thetford, and after receiving an invitation from the congregation to visit them, Madan rode over to Lakenheath and preached in the parish church.

When he was back in the village on the 26 December 1758, John Wesley heard that some of the local gentry were keen to hear him preach on condition that this was done in the parish church. He had promised to preach in Colchester the following day, but he was prepared to delay his journey. Then news came that *some hot men in the parish would not consent to my preaching there*[166] and so he moved on.

Six months later, Wesley was back at Lakenheath and was there again in February 1761 when he found a large congregation, but no organised Methodist society. He explained the need for such a society and its purpose and spoke to those who were willing to commit themselves.

John Wesley left Norwich at the end of February 1765 *in a wonderful day of frost and snow, and sleet and wind* and, after a very difficult journey, arrived at Lakenheath in the afternoon where *considering the weather, there was a large congregation*. The following morning he preached at seven and hoped to set off for London without delay, but it was *noon before we could procure a post-chaise. We then pushed on, though the snow lay deep on the ground...*[167]

On his next visit to Lakenheath, the weather once again proved difficult. Leaving Norwich on the 8 November 1770 in the pouring rain and *a*

---

[164] Ibid., iv, p.93.
[165] Martin Madan was the elder brother of the Bishop of Peterborough and the cousin of the poet William Cowper. Martin Madan had been converted by John Wesley in 1748 and was later ordained as a priest in the Church of England.
[166] Curnock, op. cit., vol. iv, p.296.
[167] Ibid., vol. v, p.107.

furious wind,[168] Wesley reached the village with difficulty and found Mr Evans *just worn out...He had not only no more strength than a little child, but no more understanding!*[169]

Mr Evans must have been on the point of death for his will was proved on 1 January 1771. He bequeathed £40 to Wesley as well as his chapel with the request that it should go on being used as a place of worship. He also directed that a parcel of his land in Mildenhall should be used to provide money to educate the children of Lakenheath.

Wesley continued to visit the village regularly until 1773. In 1771, he said he preached at Lakenheath *with an uncommon blessing.*[170] He observed that one of those who was present at the early service was Andrew Rolfe, the man who had first invited Wesley to Lakenheath fourteen years previously. Rolfe had fallen away from his faith and rarely attended the chapel, but Wesley wrote that his preaching on this occasion had reached Rolfe's heart *being in tears all the time.*[171]

To Wesley's dismay, he found that the society had vanished away when he visited Lakenheath in November 1773. He tried to encourage the members and said he would visit them again if they promised to stay together, but if not, then he had better things to do. In fact, he never did visit again.

However, it appears that although the society languished, it underwent a revival in 1787 and by 1790 had fourteen members. In 1789 it was included in the Colchester Circuit and the following year was transferred to the Bury St Edmunds Circuit which had just been created.

Loddon

10 miles south-east of Norwich

Friday 30 October 1772 – I went to Loddon...where there has been preaching for a year or two. The preaching-house at one was thoroughly filled with serious and attentive hearers.[172]

---

[168] Ibid., vol. v, p.396.
[169] Ibid.
[170] Ibid., vol. v, p.437.
[171] Ibid.
[172] Ibid., vol. v, p.486.

Friday 1 December 1786 – In the evening there seemed to be a considerable shaking even among the dry bones at Loddon; and such a company attended at Mr Crisp's in the morning as I never saw there before.[173]

*   *   *   *   *   *   *

John Wesley visited the Methodist society at Loddon on twenty occasions. He recorded that there were fifty members in 1774 and that they were *simple, teachable and all of one mind.*[174] Its leader was William Crisp, a farmer in the hamlet of Stubbs Green.[175] William Crisp and his wife, Mary, provided accommodation for the Methodist preachers on their visits. It was William Crisp who built a preaching house at Loddon in 1775, applying for a licence for it on the 24 November. It superseded the private house of Sarah and Mary Allen where the Loddon Methodists had first met around 1771-2.

Wesley mostly commented favourably on the Methodist congregation at Loddon. In 1774, he described it as *the most athirst for God of any I found in the county.*'[176]

During his visit in March 1779, he talked

> *with a girl sixteen years of age. She was justified two months since, and has not yet lost the sight of God's countenance for a moment, but has been enabled to rejoice ever more and to pray without ceasing. But being surrounded with relations who neither loved nor feared God, they were pressing upon her continually, till by little and little she sunk back into the world and had neither the power nor form of religion left.*[177]

One of the members at Loddon was Sarah Mallet.[178] John Wesley met her first at Long Stratton and wrote of this meeting as the beginning of their friendship.

The young Richard Reece, one of Wesley's itinerant preachers [ministers] was stationed in the Norwich circuit in 1788-9. Most of his work was in the area south and east of Norwich and he visited Loddon on a

---

[173] Ibid., vol. vii, p.225.
[174] Ibid., vol. vi, p.50.
[175] Stubbs Green is one mile south-west of Loddon.
[176] Curnock, op. cit., vol. vi, p.49.
[177] Ibid., vol. vi, p.223.
[178] *My Dear Sally : the Life of Sarah Mallet, one of John Wesley's Preachers*, David East, W.M.H.S., 2003, p.15. See pp.83-4.

number of occasions, staying at the house of William Crisp at Stubbs Green. In December 1788, Reece was with one of his young colleagues visiting the society at Loddon and observed in his journal that *the weather is now intensely cold; the ground is covered with snow and the air is very frosty. Our fires in general are small though we sit along with the family, not having a room to ourselves unless we go into a cold one w[h]ere one cannot stay long, so that I can write but very little...*[179]

Numbers 19-21 High Street, the first Methodist meeting place in Loddon, the home of Mary and Sarah Allen

On 16 April, Reece was once again in Loddon. He wrote of the previous evening's service; *Last night had a good season. I hope peace will be again established here, tho' it has long been the seat of contention. Bro. Freeman appears to be humbled and a much better Christian than ever he was...*[180] Quite what had prompted the quarrel and what the issues were is impossible to discover, but clearly Mr Rodwell Freeman, a tailor in the town, was one of the main protagonists.

Usually Wesley remained a few hours only at Loddon, but in October 1789, he stayed for two days, visiting the society members, conversing,

---

[179] *A Season Highly Profitable*, ed. Norma Virgoe, Wesley Historical Society East Anglia, 2007, p.22.
[180] Ibid.

praying, preaching, reading the book *Irish Antiquities* and holding a lovefeast.

His last visit was in October 1790 when he travelled to Stubbs Green in a chaise with the itinerant preacher, Joseph Bradford. By this time he was 87 and it was felt that he was too old and frail to travel on his extensive tours alone. After lunch, he went on to the Loddon chapel where he preached his final sermon in the little town. By four o'clock, he was back in Norwich.

Long Stratton

10 miles south of Norwich

Monday 4 December 1786 – I was strongly importuned by our friends at Long Stratton to give them a sermon there. I heard of a young woman in that country who had uncommon fits, and of one that had lately preached; but I did not know that it was one and the same person. I found her in the very house to which I went, and went and talked with her at large. I was surprised Sarah Mallet, two or three and twenty years old, is of the same size that Jane Cooper was;[181] *and is, I think, full as much devoted to God and as of strong an understanding. But she is not likely to live, having a species of consumption which I believe is never cured. Of the following relation which she gave me, there are numberless witnesses.*

Some years since, it was strongly impressed upon her that she ought to call sinners to repentance. This impression she vehemently resisted, believing herself quite unqualified, both by her sin and her ignorance, till it was suggested, "if you do it not willingly, you shall do it whether you will or no." She fell into a fit and, while utterly senseless, thought she was in the preaching-house in Lowestoft, where she prayed and preached for near an hour to a numerous congregation. She then opened her eyes and recovered her senses. In a year or two, she had eighteen of these fits, in every one of which she imagined herself to be preaching in one or another congregation. She then cried out, "Lord, I will obey Thee; I will call sinners to repentance." She has done so occasionally from that time; and her fits returned no more.[182]

---

[181] Jane Cooper spoke in London and was criticised by some men for doing so. *She Offered Them Christ*, Paul Chilcote, 1993, Abingdon Press, p.54.

[182] Curnock, op. cit., vol. vii, pp.226-7.

* * * * * * *

John Wesley was clearly fascinated by Sarah Mallet's story. One of several Norfolk women preachers, she exercised her ministry in many of the Norfolk towns and villages. She must have heard Mary Sewell, a Methodist local preacher and a near neighbour, speak in public and later she befriended another young woman, Elizabeth Reeve, who also felt a call to preach.

Sarah Mallet began to preach in February 1786, speaking first at North Lopham and then every other week at the house of her uncle, William Mallet, in Long Stratton and as a result, found peace of mind. She looked to John Wesley as her spiritual guide and director. He, for his part, was convinced of her gift and he secured for her an authorisation to preach from the 1787 Conference. He wrote many letters to guide and counsel her, sent books for her instruction and edification and gave advice as to how to behave towards the male itinerant preachers. John Wesley's support helped to diminish opposition to her work.

Sarah worked as a tailor, like so many of her family, and in this way she made sure she did not have to rely on other people financially. She was also sent money by John Wesley to help her continue her preaching work. He wrote,

> *I know that neither your father nor uncle is rich; and in travelling up and down you will want a little money. Are you not sometimes straightened? Only let me know, and you shall want nothing.*[183]

When John Wesley visited Long Stratton in 1786, he stayed at William Mallet's house. By this time, there was a Methodist society of eleven members with William as its leader. It is said that the Methodist society first met in the most northerly of three cottages next to St Mary's churchyard.[184]

In 1777, a barn belonging to John Haken of Wacton was licensed for Methodist worship. It was situated behind the cottages in a yard next to the churchyard and was used by William Mallet. It continued to be used as a place of worship until 1829 when a chapel was built.

Wesley was in Long Stratton for the last time in 1789, once again staying in William Mallet's house.

---

[183] *Letters* Telford, op. cit., vol. viii, pp.43-4.
[184] *The Spreading Flame*, Cyril Jolly, n.d., p.65.

Lowestoft

22 miles south-east of Norwich and 8 miles south of Great Yarmouth

Thursday 11 October 1764 – I was desired to go to Lowestoft in Suffolk...I preached in the open air. A wilder congregation I had not seen, but the bridle was in their teeth. All attended, and a considerable part seemed to understand something of what was spoken. Nor did any behave uncivilly when I had done.[185]

*   *   *   *   *   *   *

Four Lowestoft men, Thomas Tripp, a cooper, Samuel and John Farrar, twine spinners, and William Butcher, went to Yarmouth in 1762 to hear one of John Wesley's itinerant preachers, John Pawson. What they heard convinced them of their need for salvation and so they invited John Pawson and another itinerant, Daniel Bumstead, to preach at Lowestoft.

A society was formed, but the Methodists met with much violent opposition. Mrs Alice Ibrook with whom the preachers lodged, had her windows broken and her grocer's shop was damaged. Threats were made against others who allowed preaching in their houses and Thomas Tripp was stoned in the street.

In spite of this hostility, stables next to the Blue Anchor Inn were furnished as a chapel and the congregation was greatly helped on a number of occasions by Thomas Tripp who had become a local preacher and had married the widowed Mrs Ibrook.

John Wesley made sixteen visits to the town. He usually came to Lowestoft from Yarmouth, returning the same day, although this was not always so. On his first visit in 1764, it was expected that he would preach in the Independent meeting house which had been borrowed for the occasion. However, it appeared that one of the trustees feared possible violence which could cause damage and so John Wesley found the meeting house closed to him. Instead, he was compelled to preach out of doors.

The Methodist preacher, John Brownell, wrote of this visit,

It is highly probable that the presence of so venerable a person restrained the multitude; his flowing eloquence charmed their ears, as well as affected their hearts; but with all his superior

---

[185] Curnock, op. cit., vol. v, p.99.

advantages, he only just escaped being insulted, for the people were ready for mischief ...But the rage of persecution which like a torrent... soon after rushed forth with redoubled force.[186]

One of the stalwart Lowestoft members was Thomas Mallet. A very knowledgeable man, he was fluent in Hebrew, Greek and Latin and John Wesley found him a very congenial companion. Adam Clarke, one of Wesley's preachers, was also impressed with Thomas Mallet and wrote of his extensive Biblical scholarship and his kindness and acknowledged that he had been a very great help in guiding Clarke's studies. He described Thomas Mallet and Thomas Tripp as *eyes to the blind and feet to the lame.*[187]

On 19 November 1776, Wesley opened a new preaching house there. He described it as a *lightsome building.*[188] It was a plain brick chapel with a small gallery at one end and cost £300. Thomas Tripp donated £50 of this sum and a similar amount was given by Samuel Farrar, another of the group who had originally gone to hear John Pawson in Yarmouth so long before.

The following morning, Wesley's travelling companion, the Rev. John Fletcher, who had been advised to travel for the good of his health, preached in the new chapel whilst John Wesley spoke in the afternoon.

> *It then blew a thorough storm so that it was hard to walk or stand, the wind being ready to take us off our feet. It drove one of the boats which were on the strand from its moorings out to sea. Three men were in it, who looked for nothing every moment but to be swallowed up. But presently, five stout men put off in another open boat and, rowing for life, overtook them and brought them safe to land.*[189]

In March 1779, John Wesley reported *a great awakening* at Lowestoft. *especially among youth and children; several of whom, between twelve and sixteen years of age are a pattern to all about them.*[190]

---

[186] *Wesleyan Methodist Magazine*, 1811, p.149.
[187] Quoted in 'A Short History of Lowestoft Methodism, 1762-1951', no author or date, Lowestoft Record Office, 47/E1/1.
[188] Curnock, op. cit., vol. vi, p.132.
[189] Ibid.
[190] Ibid., vol. vi, p.223.

Writing to the army commander in the town on 30 November 1782, Wesley complained that his officers were disturbing Methodist worship.[191]

By 1785, there were fifty members belonging to the Lowestoft society listed in the circuit book. By 1792, this number had risen to ninety-three.[192] These included a number of shoe makers and painters as well as other tradesmen: bricklayers, carpenters, tailors, milliners and a hat maker, a cutler and several servants. Not surprisingly some members were engaged in employments relating to the sea: two sea captains, sailors, a sail maker, shipwrights and a bargeman as well as a customs-house officer. There were also two school masters and a printer.

In October 1788, Richard Reece, one of the young itinerant preachers, accompanied John Wesley on his visit to Lowestoft. Reece noted in his journal, *The people here have the appearance of hospitality. The companies are large where Mr Wesley goes and love seems to reign amongst them universally.*[193]

Wesley's last visit to the town was in October 1790. On this occasion, the poet George Crabbe was present in the chapel and heard him preach. Crabbe's son, who was also present, described John Wesley as *exceedingly old and infirm and [he] was attended, almost supported in the pulpit by a young minister on each side.*[194] The church was filled to a point of near suffocation. Crabbe remarked on Wesley's dignified demeanour, his cheerfulness and the musical way he declaimed some poetic lines of the ancient Greek lyric poet, Anacreon, adapting them to his own person;

> *Oft am I by women told,*
> *Poor John Wesley! Thou grow'st old;*
> *See, thine hairs are falling all:*
> *Poor John Wesley! How they fall!*
> *Whether I grow old or no,*
> *By these signs I do not know;*
> *But this I need not to be told,*
> *'Tis time to <u>live</u>, if I grow old.*[195]

After the sermon, the elder George Crabbe introduced himself to Wesley, *the patriarch, who received him with benevolent politeness.*[196]

---

[191] *Letters*, Telford, op. cit., vol. vii, pp.151-2.
[192] N.R.O., FC 16/1, op. cit.
[193] Virgoe, op. cit., p.15.
[194] *The Poetical Works of the Rev, George Crabbe*, George Crabbe jun., 1834, London, vol.i, p.148.
[195] Ibid.

Newmarket

13 miles west of Bury St Edmunds

Friday 19 July 1754 – I rode to Newmarket and the next day to Bedford.[197]

* * * * * * *

This brief entry in his journal records John Wesley's first visit to Newmarket. He was returning from Norwich where he had been able to speak only a few words to the assembled crowds. Still weak after a prolonged illness, he left Charles in Norwich and set out for Newmarket where he stayed the night. Riding to Bedford the next day, he felt well enough to preach there and then went on to London.

In 1759, after spending two days in Bedford, Wesley rode to Newmarket and then went on to Norwich the following day.

He again spent the night in the town on his way to Norwich at the end of November 1769.

He was next in Newmarket on 20 October 1783, arriving at the coaching halt early in the morning, taking tea and reading a Shakespeare play. He was there briefly again ten days later when returning from King's Lynn to London, this time reading Thomas Baker's *Reflections upon Learning.*[198] As usual, he drank morning tea before taking the London coach.

The following year, he reached Newmarket at six in the morning from London, had tea and then went on to Norwich. He did the same in October 1785. His last visit to the town saw him arrive there from London at 4.30 in the morning on the 1 October 1788 on his way to King's Lynn.

All of Wesley's journeys through Newmarket were accomplished safely and without mishap, although the threat from highwaymen was far greater on this road than the route from Colchester and Ipswich.

Although he was usually in Newmarket in October when the town was thronged with race-goers, at no time does he mention that he preached nor had any significant conversation there. He never mentions any Methodists or any religious gatherings. Newmarket appears simply to have been a convenient place to stop and rest on his way to visit other places.

---

[196] Ibid.
[197] Curnock, op. cit., vol. iv, p.96.
[198] *Reflections on Learning, showing the Insufficiency thereof in its Several Particulars, in order to evince the Usefulness and Necessity of Revelation,* Thomas Baker, 1709-10, London.

North Cove

18 miles south-east of Norwich and 7 miles south-west of Lowestoft

Saturday 2 November 1782 – I preached at [North] Cove, a village nine or ten miles from Lowestoft; the poor people presently filled the house and seemed to devour every word.[199]

* * * * * * *

John Wesley visited North Cove on another five occasions. He usually arrived from Lowestoft in the morning and after refreshing himself with tea, preached to *an earnest, lively people.*[200] Then he left again, often to travel on to Loddon.

This very small village had a Methodist society of thirty-eight members in 1785. This number included three woodmen, two farmers and a dauber.[201] The following year, more occupations of the members were given and these were listed as a shoe maker, husbandmen, farmer's wife, a shopkeeper, three housewives and two women who were living with their parents.

Scole

1 mile east of Diss and 19 miles south-south-east of Norwich

Monday 24 December 1759 – We did not set out till after seven intending to ride about forty miles; but, coming to Scole Inn before three, we pushed on and before seven came safe to Norwich.[202]

* * * * * * *

Coming from Colchester at Christmas 1759, John Wesley rode north on the turnpike road to Scole on the Norfolk-Suffolk border. The road was on the line of an old Roman road.

The Scole Inn, also known as the White Hart Inn, was a posting stage on the road from Ipswich to Norwich. It had been built in 1655 by James Peck,

---

[199] Curnock, op. cit., vol. vi. pp.376-7.
[200] Ibid, vol. vi, p.457.
[201] N.R.O., FC 16/1, op. cit. A 'dauber' was a plasterer.
[202] Curnock, op. cit., vol. iv, p.362-3.

a rich Norwich merchant whose ambition was to build the very finest inn in England. His design was most elaborate with decorated gables in the seventeenth-century Dutch style and much carved and moulded brick work. However, its most notable feature was a huge and magnificent sign which stretched right across the road. It had been created by an artist Johannes Fairchild and cost the enormous sum of £1057.

In the centre of the sign stood a large white hart. To one side was displayed the goddess Diana hunting with dogs and huntsmen. On the other side was a man with the horned head of a deer who appeared to be Actaeon being changed by Diana into a stag. Other figures portrayed lions, dogs, a figure of Bacchus, another representing Justice as well as a number of winged spirits. A weather vane was also incorporated into the display. It showed a seated astronomer who faced towards the point of the compass from which rain was coming in wet weather and in fine weather faced towards the north. In addition to these life-size figures, there was also a collection of coats of arms. The sign was removed about the year 1800.

The Scole Inn

The inn offered hospitality to travellers on the road. In 1683, King Charles II had briefly stopped there to eat breakfast when on his way to Yarmouth. With the improvement of the road and the consequent considerable increase in coach traffic, the inn became popular with travellers seeking food and a change of horses. The inn was also renowned for its great bed which could hold thirty to forty people. The bed was kept in an outhouse and was used for vagrants and other poor travellers. In the garden behind the inn, cock fights were often held.

John Wesley, however, on this Christmas Eve, did not take advantage of the inn's convivial welcome.

Stoke-by-Clare

15 miles south-south-east of Bury St Edmunds and 27 miles west of Ipswich

*   *   *   *   *   *   *

Tuesday 5 January 1762 – In the afternoon we set out for Stoke on the edge of Suffolk...All was quiet at Stoke for Sir H...A...will suffer no disturbance there. The congregation came from many miles round and God was in the midst of them. Thus hearty prayers went up on every side. And many felt the answer to them.

Wednesday 6 January 1762 – The largeness of the congregation at five showed they were not forgetful hearers. I preached longer than I am accustomed to do, but still they were not satisfied. Many crowded after me into the dwelling house. After speaking a few words, I went to prayer. A cry began and soon spread through the whole company, so that my voice was lost. Two seemed to be distressed above all the rest. We continued wrestling with God till one of them had a good hope, and the other was 'filled with joy and peace in believing.[203]

*   *   *   *   *   *   *

On his way to Stoke-by-Clare, John Wesley had received a noisy reception from the mob at Haverhill. Things were calmer in this village. Alderman Sir Henry Archer, knight, of Saffron Walden, had lands in Stoke-by-Clare where he obviously exerted a strong hold.

It is not clear why John Wesley came to this area of Suffolk on the extreme south-west border of the county. There was no mention of someone he wished to visit. Neither was it a place of high population such as usually attracted Wesley.

---

[203] Ibid., vol. iv, pp.483-4.

Wesley does not say where he addressed the crowds who came to hear him in Stoke-by-Clare. There was no Methodist meeting house here at this time so perhaps he preached in the open air.

Stoke Ferry

14 miles south-east of King's Lynn

*   *   *   *   *   *   *

John Wesley's only visit here was during his last tour of the county. After spending a couple of days in Lynn where he opened the new preaching house and where he was the guest of one of the clergy of St Margaret's church, the Rev. Edward Edwards, he set off for Diss on Wednesday 20 October 1790. He left Lynn shortly after four in the morning in a chaise with Joseph Bradford and Thomas Tattershall. Joseph Bradford had been appointed to travel with the aged Wesley in the years 1787-90 whilst Tattershall was one of the itinerant preachers stationed in the Lynn circuit in 1790.

The road the men travelled along was the turnpike between Lynn and Thetford. They changed carriages at Stoke Ferry, but there is no evidence that Wesley preached here.

A house was licensed in Stoke Ferry for Methodist preaching the following year and the society was incorporated into the King's Lynn circuit.

The Methodist itinerant preacher, Joseph Bradford, was a devoted friend of John Wesley. He was one of the group of Wesley's closest companions who stood round his deathbed.

Swaffham

26 miles west of Norwich

Monday 18 October 1790 – No coach going out for Lynn today [from Norwich], *I was obliged to take a post-chaise. But at Dereham no horses were to be had; so we were obliged to take the same horses to Swaffham. A congregation was ready here, that filled the house, and seemed quite ready to receive instruction. But here neither could we procure any post-horses; so that we were obliged to take a single-horse chaise. The wind, with mizzling rain, came full in our faces, and we had nothing to screen us from it; so that I was thoroughly chilled from head to foot before I came to Lynn.*[204]

$$\ast \quad \ast \quad \ast \quad \ast \quad \ast \quad \ast \quad \ast$$

In January 1772, *a dwelling house consisting of two low rooms* was licensed for religious worship for Methodists in Swaffham.[205] The house was owned by Robert Goodrick, a leather cutter, and his wife, Mary, and occupied a corner plot on London Street and the Pightle. Two years later, they applied for another licence for a house belonging to them. Then in 1775, they registered an outhouse attached to their house which was called 'the Leather House.'

John Wesley's first visit on Friday 3 October 1788 was a transitory one. After spending two days in Lynn, he took the stage coach at 7 am and set out for Norwich. At ten o'clock, he arrived at Swaffham where his diary records that he took tea, conversed, prayed and then took the coach for the next stage of his journey.

His second visit in 1790 was not much longer. He arrived in Swaffham from Dereham at 11.45 am, preached at midday, dined with Robert Goodrick and then set out for Lynn, arriving there at 5 pm.

Tradition has it that John Wesley delivered one sermon from a window in Robert Goodrick's house and another one *to an uproarious crowd on Market Hill where he was pelted with garbage, rotten eggs and stones, many windows being broken.*[206] Nothing of this appears in Wesley's journal

---

[204] Ibid., vol. viii, p.107.
[205] N.R.O., DN/DIS, 1/2, op. cit.
[206] *Our Town: being a sketch, historical, descriptive and ecclesiastical of the town of Swaffham in Norfolk*, William Castell Southwell, 1892, Swaffham, p.26.

or diary of this tumult and he records preaching only one sermon in the town inside the house to a receptive congregation.

Plaque on Robert Goodrick's house

Thetford

29 miles south-west of Norwich

Thursday 24 November 1757 – A man had spoken to me the last week as I was going through Thetford and desired me to preach at Lakenheath...I now purposed so to do and rode thither from Thetford[207]

*   *   *   *   *   *   *

John Wesley rode through Thetford on his way to and from Norwich on this and other occasions, but he does not appear to have preached in the town.

The section of the turnpike which ran through Thetford to Norwich also passed through Attleborough and Wymondham, but there is no record of him preaching in these towns either.

---

[207] Curnock, op. cit., vol. iv, pp.244-5.

However on Wednesday 20 October 1790, during the course of his final visit to Norfolk, Wesley stopped briefly in Thetford on his way from Lynn to Diss. Arriving at 10 in the morning, he left again just half an hour later.

Nevertheless by this time, there was a Methodist presence in Thetford. A small group of people had invited itinerant preachers from the Colchester Circuit to come and preach to them. In response, Samuel Gates travelled to Thetford and preached a sermon about the Day of Judgement. From time to time, other preachers were invited and these included Sarah Mallet who was described as *a very useful woman* who *attracted great attention*.[208]

On 6 January 1791, the Thetford Methodists were organised into a formal society of eight members by the itinerant preacher, Thomas Broadbent, and regular services began. The Thetford society was incorporated into the Bury St Edmunds Circuit and met in the thatched cottage of one of the members. It was during that first quarter that Thomas Broadbent preached a funeral sermon for John Wesley to the Thetford congregation.[209]

Thurlton

5 miles north of Beccles

Although John Wesley never visited Thurlton, the village was not unknown to him. A number of women, he discovered, had been preaching in Norfolk, some of them with the Methodists, and he came to know several of them. One was Mary Sewell, who, in the circuit book begun in 1785, was listed as a local preacher in the Norwich circuit and leader of the class at Thurlton.

She preached to many of the Methodist societies in south-east Norfolk and north-east Suffolk with great effect and on one occasion, braved the hostility of the mob at Yarmouth. One of those who heard her was William Lamb, the uncle of the itinerant preacher, Charles Atmore.[210]

Someone else who heard her with great interest and approval was another of Wesley's itinerants, Adam Clarke. As a young man, he was stationed in the Norwich Circuit and was initially averse to the idea of

---

[208] Letter written by William Oldman to James Fison, 1840, and quoted in 'Memories of Thetford and Troston' by Joseph Howard in the *Methodist Recorder*, 27 March 1890.
[209] Ibid.
[210] See pp.63-5.

women preachers. However, his views were modified by hearing Mary preach. He wrote,

> *I have this morning heard Miss Sewell preach; she has a good talent for exhortation, and her words spring from a heart that evidently feels deep concern for the souls of the people; and, consequently, her hearers are interested and affected. I have formerly been no friend to female preaching; but my sentiments are a little altered. If God give [sic] to a holy woman a gift for exhortation and reproof, I see no reason why it should not be used. This woman's preaching has done much good; and fruits of it may be found copiously, in different places in the circuit.*[211]

After undertaking a great deal of preaching work stretching over two years, Mary Sewell died in October 1786.

In Thurlton, the house of Simon Crisp, a farmer and known Methodist, was licensed for religious worship on 10 June 1775. Then, the following month, he applied for a worship certificate for his barn. Perhaps the numbers attending services were too large to be accommodated in the farmhouse.

Walpole Cross Keys

8 miles west of King's Lynn

Monday 2 April 1759 – I left Norwich and about seven o'clock came to Cross-Keys Wash. They would fain have persuaded us we could not pass; but finding we were resolved to try, our guide put forward and brought us over in half an hour; so that about eight we reached Sutton and found a quiet civil house with everything we wanted.[212]

*   *   *   *   *   *   *

Walpole Cross Keys was set in the area known as Marshland, a landscape covered by cuts, drains and ditches and with salt marshes stretching to the sea. The River Nene wound its way through this watery

---

[211] From the journal of Adam Clarke, quoted in ed. J.B.B. Clarke, *An Account of the Life of Adam Clarke*, 1833, London, vol. i, pp.215-16.
[212] Curnock, op. cit., vol. iv, p.304.

area and formed the boundary between Norfolk and Lincolnshire. The land was crossed by three main ways. The most northerly of these routes came west from Lynn, through the parishes of Clenchwarton and Terrington St Clement to Walpole Cross Keys. From there it became a precarious and dangerous track with the Wash Way, a sunken causeway two miles long, crossing the county boundary and leading to Sutton Bridge. The causeway which ran across first the salt marsh and then a sandy arm of the Wash, was flooded and impassable at high tide and could only be used when the tide was low when it became almost dry. A number of lives had been lost attempting to cross here and it was widely regarded as a very dangerous crossing. Clearly Wesley's impatience to hurry on led him to make a foolhardy decision to cross the inundated land before it was safe to do so.

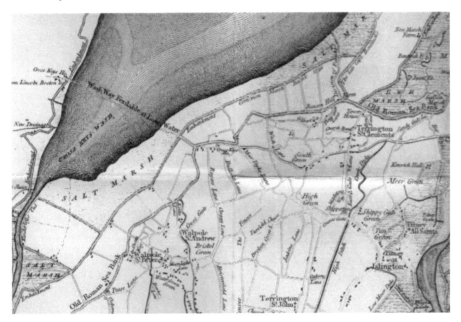

William Faden's map of north-west Norfolk, 1796
showing the two-mile causeway across the Wash

On his journey, John Wesley would have seen the huge mediaeval parish churches so characteristic of this part of Norfolk and built from the wealth generated by the sheep that still thickly dotted the grassland of this rich landscape.

Little Walsingham

25 miles north-west of Norwich and 4 miles north of Fakenham

Tuesday 30 October 1781 – At two in the afternoon I preached at Walsingham, a place famous for many generations. Afterwards I walked over what is left of the famous Abbey, the east end of which is still standing. We then went to the Friary, the cloister and chapel whereof are almost entire. Had there been a grain of virtue or public spirit in Henry the Eighth, these noble buildings need not have run to ruin.[213]

*   *   *   *   *   *   *

About the year 1150, Richelde of Ferraques saw in a dream the house of the Annunciation in Nazareth. She constructed a copy of this house at Walsingham. Her son, on his return from a pilgrimage to the Holy Land, built a priory for Augustinian canons on the same site. Visited by both Henry III and Edward I, it quickly became one of the most popular pilgrimage sites and the priory was one of the richest in England.

The Abbey gatehouse

---

[213] Ibid.,vol. vi, p.339.

The Grey Friars founded a church in 1347 at the south end of the village. The ruins now stand in the grounds of a private house. The original guest house of the complex largely survives and so too does a little cloister. The large cloister has the present garden set out within its walls. Very little now remains of the chapel mentioned by John Wesley.

Although it was not recorded by Wesley, a Methodist society was formed in 1779 and so was in existence when he visited the little town. Its first chapel was built in 1782. It was a small building which later became two cottages.[214] A new Methodist chapel was built in the village in 1793-4. It is now the oldest surviving Methodist chapel in East Anglia[1] which is still used for worship.

Wells-next-the-Sea

23 miles north-east of King's Lynn and 9 miles north of Fakenham

Tuesday 30 October 1781 – I went to Wells, a considerable seaport... where also Miss Franklin had opened a door, by preaching abroad, though at the peril of her life. She was followed by a young woman of the town, with whom I talked largely, and found her very sensible, and much devoted to God. From her I learnt that, till the Methodists came, they had none but female teachers in this country; and that there were six of these within ten or twelve miles, all of whom were members of the Church of England. I preached about ten in a small, neat preaching-house; And all but two or three were very attentive.[215]

        *   *   *   *   *   *   *

John Wesley must have been surprised to hear that in this part of the country, several women had been active in teaching and preaching the good news of the Gospel.

These women, led by Mary Franklin,[216] had set up a Calvinist meeting in Wells and established classes similar to the Methodist class meetings in several of the surrounding villages as well as in Wells itself. From what

---

[214] One cottage was rented by a shepherd and then a widow and one of the cottages was eventually turned into a stable for the minister's horse – Jolly, op. cit., p.76.
[215] Curnock, op. cit., vol. vi, pp.338-9.
[216] See pp..57-9.

Wesley wrote, it sounded as though they had experienced considerable opposition and danger at times.

Almost two years before Wesley's visit, an application for a religious licence was made on 1 January 1789 for a chapel in the town. The application states that the preaching house was *late fitted up for the purpose*[217] and it was here that John Wesley preached on his visit to Wells-next-the-Sea.

John Wesley had been invited to Wells by John Keed, an attender of the Calvinist congregation there. Keed had travelled to King's Lynn in order to hear John Wesley preach and after the service, had spoken to Wesley and told him about the disputes which were wracking the congregation in Wells. Wesley agreed to visit the town and, in consequence, a Methodist society was soon set up.

Keed offered his hospitality to the Methodist preachers, helping them to start causes in many villages and sometimes suffering with them the violent attacks of hostile crowds. He also aided them financially. He moved to Lynn in 1781 and continued his support for Methodism there.

In 1779, two years before John Wesley's visit, John Pritchard, one of the Methodist itinerant preachers, was stationed in the King's Lynn Circuit. At this time, the circuit stretched eastwards to Wells, Walsingham and south to Fakenham. He wrote in his memoirs that in those towns

> *and many of the villages, we gathered many into Societies who were careless and wicked before. But in the towns along the sea-coast we met with much trouble, especially from the smugglers. We applied to the justices, who were more afraid of them than we were; and who told us, if we would preach on Sundays, they would protect us, but not on other days.*[218]

John Wesley was rigorous in opposing smuggling. It was, however, widely prevalent in eighteenth-century England and regarded by most people as a minor misdemeanour only. People were ready to receive smuggled goods in spite of government attempts to prevent the trade and very heavy penalties for those who were caught. Even some of the clergy were involved; James Woodforde, rector of Weston Longville, recorded in his diary a number of deliveries of tea and Indian silk handkerchiefs, as well as barrels of gin and rum and he took them with an easy conscience.

---

[217] NRO DN DIS 1/2, op. cit.
[218]*The Early Methodist Preachers*, Thomas Jackson, 5th edition, London: Wesleyan Methodist Book Room, vol. vi, pp.267-8.

He was by no means the only Norfolk parson to connive in the trade. For years the rector's barn at Waxham was used to store smuggled goods and the parson was rewarded with kegs of spirits.

John Wesley described smuggling as *an accursed thing*,[219] and spoke against it all round the coast. It was discussed at the 1767 Conference and preachers were urged to expel from societies those who received smuggled items and to distribute Wesley's pamphlet, *A Word to a Smuggler* as widely as possible. In the pamphlet, Wesley described smugglers as thieves who were picking the pockets of the king as well as every honest man.

Accosting smugglers was a dangerous venture. Smugglers were armed and some gangs were large. They were ready to kill those who opposed them and it was often necessary to enlist the aid of soldiers to strengthen the work of the preventive men. Open fights between soldiers and smugglers often led to loss of life on both sides.

Several licences for religious worship were issued for various premises in Wells in the early 1780s, but there is no indication as to the denomination of the people applying. However, a licence sought on the 13 May 1786 for *a certain house formerly used as an Engine House* by William Weldrile of Wells, *officer of Excise*[220] was certainly intended for a Methodist place of worship. William Weldrile was a known and committed Methodist and he applied for a number of religious licences for premises in villages in north Norfolk.

Another member of this Methodist society was Mary Proudfoot. She was one of the women who had worked with Mary Franklin in her preaching endeavours in north Norfolk in the 1770s and early 1780s and who was mentioned by John Wesley in one of his letters to Mary Franklin. It is likely that it was she who was *the young woman of the town* who met and spoke to John Wesley during his visit to Wells-next-the-Sea in 1781.

Yarmouth

19 miles east of Norwich

John Wesley's first visit to Yarmouth was on Tuesday 20 January 1761. He had enquired about the town whilst he was in Norwich and heard that it

---

[219] Curnock, op. cit., vol. vi, p.6.
[220] NRO, DN/DIS 1/2, op. cit.

101

was *a large and populous town and as eminent both for wickedness and ignorance as even any seaport in England.*[221]

Wesley was not the first Methodist to visit Yarmouth. In 1754, Thomas Olivers, an itinerant preacher from Norwich had attempted to preach in the market place, but was met by a noisy and hostile reception and when pelted with a hail of dirt and stones, made his escape back to Norwich vowing never to return.

A further effort was made to mission the town in 1760. Howell Harris, a Welshman, a soldier and a Methodist who was stationed with his regiment in the town, resolved to preach to the people. Expecting hostility, he arranged for the town crier to announce that a Methodist preacher might be heard in the market place. An excited crowd gathered armed with missiles.

Thomas Olivers

Shortly before the time appointed, Captain Harris appeared with some of his soldiers and drilled them in sight of the people. Hearing from the crowd the reason why they were gathered there, he said that as the preacher had not turned up, he would talk to them instead. He climbed on a table and with his soldiers surrounding him with bayonets fixed, he sang a hymn and preached to the fascinated and surprised crowd.

Harris preached again on subsequent evenings and clearly some people were sympathetic for they sent a message in 1761 to John Wesley in Norwich begging him to visit the town. He found a quiet and substantial congregation ready to hear him.

---

[221] Curnock, op. cit., vol. iv, p.431.

William Lilly, 1602-81

An astrologer who was consulted by Charles I, he predicted the Great Fire of London fourteen years before it happened. He was put on trial for deliberately starting the fire, but with no evidence to support the accusation, he was declared innocent. John Wesley read his autobiography whilst at Yarmouth in 1763 and commented, 'Was ever man so deluded?'[222]

Two years later, Wesley again visited the town and had many hearers. By 1764, the Methodists were renting a Baptist chapel for worship. When Wesley preached there in February 1765, he described it as *one of the most elegant buildings I have seen which was well filled...with serious and attentive hearers.*[223]

This was the calm before the storm. Benjamin Worship, a Yarmouth lawyer and Methodist local preacher suddenly became a fervent Calvinist. He was a persuasive and forceful influence and his activities tore the Methodists apart. Attracting a significant following, he took over the chapel and most of the congregation for himself.

John Wesley tried to organise and enthuse those who were left, but arriving in Yarmouth in December 1767, he *found confusion worse confounded.*[224] The congregation had ceased attending services at the parish church, was full of criticisms of the clergy and were quarrelling with each other. Wesley struggled to reconcile them and resolve the difficulties, insisting the Methodists should remain within the Church of England and attend services at the parish church.

Travelling to the town in February 1769, he had to contend with heavy rain and a very bad road. The journey from Bury St Edmunds took him eleven hours on horseback and he arrived tired and soaked, but preached to a large congregation, the largest he had yet encountered in the town. Yet

---

[222] Ibid., vol. v. pp.36-7.
[223] Ibid., vol. v, p.107.
[224] Ibid., vol. v, p.245.

eight months later on his next visit, he found it *a cold, dead, uncomfortable place.*[225]

A further theological dispute shattered the congregation in 1774 so that a mere handful of members was left. When Wesley visited the town in 1776, he hoped to preach in the town hall. At the last minute, the Mayor changed his mind and refused permission. However, the town Chamberlain came to the rescue and allocated a larger building which had once been the Dutch church. Although there was a large congregation, it appears that no formal Methodist society then existed.

In 1780, James Wood, a preacher stationed in the Norwich circuit visited Samuel King, a Yarmouth brazier and former Methodist, who had continued to hold simple services at his house for his neighbours. King borrowed the General Baptist church for Wood's visit and as a result, a regular group led by King began to meet at various cottages in the town. By the time of Wesley's next visit in October 1781, a new Methodist society of seventeen members had been formed. A year later, the number had grown to sixty-two, divided into five classes.

A Yarmouth corn merchant, Mr Lee, gave a piece of land and a quantity of bricks, money was collected, including £100 from John Wesley, and a chapel was built in Ferry Boat Row, North Quay. It cost £315 and seated 500 people and was opened by Wesley himself in 1783. It was known as 'Fish Chapel.' John Wesley wrote,

> *Wednesday 22 October 1783 – I went to Yarmouth. Often this poor society had been wellnigh shattered in pieces; first by Benjamin Worship, then a furious Calvinist, tearing away near half of them; next by John Simpson turning Antinomian and scattering most that were left. It has pleased God, contrary to all human probability, to raise a new society out of the dust; nay, and to give them courage to build a new preaching-house, which is well finished and contains about five hundred persons. I opened it this evening; and as many as could get in seemed to be deeply affected. Who knows but God is about to repair the waste places and to gather a people that shall be scattered no more?*[226]

Shortly afterwards James Hindmarsh, one of the Methodist itinerant preachers, retired to Yarmouth and his presence in the town seemed to

[225] Ibid., vol. v, p.347.
[226] Ibid., vol. vi, pp.455-6.

suggest a bright future for Methodism as he continued to preach and lead classes. Quickly, however, two factions formed with Hindmarsh refusing to remain in chapel when Samuel King took services. Soon King was left with very few friends although he had done much good work, giving hospitality to the visiting itinerant preachers and taking on responsibility for building the chapel. Wesley, too, viewed him as a sensible and dedicated man.

King, not wishing to be the cause of disruption amongst the congregation, stopped attending services, leaving Hindmarsh triumphant. Soon, however, Hindmarsh left Yarmouth and renounced his Methodist opinions. King was persuaded to rejoin the Methodist society.

In October 1790, John Wesley made his twenty-eighth and last visit to Yarmouth and found a united society. In the evening, the congregation was too large to get into the preaching-house. Wesley wrote, *after supper a little company went to prayer and the power of God fell upon us; especially when a young woman broke out into prayer, to the surprise and comfort of us all.*[227]

After all his efforts at Yarmouth, he was clearly pleased and relieved to find the congregation settled, devoted and flourishing at last.

Travelling

Thursday 16 February 1769 – Supposing we had but five-and-forty miles to Yarmouth (from Bury St Edmunds), *I did not set out till near seven. But it proved three-score; likewise it rained all day, and a part of the road was very bad. However, God strengthened both man and beast, so we reached it before six in the evening.*[228]

*   *   *   *   *   *   *

By the beginning of the eighteenth century, turnpike trusts began to be established by Acts of Parliament as the result of local initiatives. This measure enabled tolls from travellers to be used for the improvement and upkeep of the roads and relieved this burdensome task from parishes through which the roads passed.

A list of toll charges was advertised on toll boards at toll houses. A number of exemptions allowed marching soldiers, electors going to the

---

[227] Ibid., vol. viii, p.106.
[228] Ibid., vol, v, p.300.

polls to vote, church attenders and those in charge of farm traffic to pass freely along the road. Clergy were also exempt from charges so John Wesley would have been able to travel without paying toll charges.

The first turnpikes were roads which already existed rather than new constructions. Gates or bars were put across the roads and toll keepers were appointed to collect the dues.

Toll house on the Thetford-to-Norwich turnpike road.
The house is set at an angle to the road so that the road can be observed in both directions and approaching travellers easily seen. The large number of windows allows a number of different observation points.

In 1696, one of the first turnpike trusts was established for the road between Wymondham and Attleborough, although it was not until 1767 that the Bill for making the whole of the road between Town Close in Norwich to Thetford received the Royal assent.

In 1711-12, the first Suffolk turnpike was set up on the Ipswich-to-Scole road. Many roads were designated turnpikes in Suffolk in the 1760s and 1770s whilst in Norfolk there was an intense burst of applications between 1769 and 1772.

In 1744, an Act of Parliament ordered that milestones should be placed on most roads. In 1766, the General Turnpike Act made them compulsory on all turnpike roads and so milestones were set up by the controlling turnpike trust on that section of the road.

The great improvement in the state of the roads meant that journeys could be accomplished far more speedily and time spent on the roads was greatly reduced. It also went hand in hand with a proliferation in the choice of types of transport available to travellers.

John Wesley was renowned for the immense number of miles he covered on horseback. On some of his earlier visits to East Anglia, he mentioned in his journal that he rode there. However, for the first time in October 1764, he wrote that he took 'the machine'[229] on his journey from London to Yarmouth via Bury St Edmunds.

The 'Norwich Machine' set out from the Maid's Head Inn next to the Cathedral precinct in Norwich at half past ten in the morning on Mondays, Wednesdays and Fridays each week. It carried four inside passengers as well as several outside travellers. The inside passengers were allowed luggage *of twenty pounds weight ... to be paid for at three half pence per pound* and the travellers *to be in London on the Tuesday, Thursday and Saturday evenings*, a lengthy and tiring journey.[230] In 1784 the 'Expedition' took over from the 'Norwich Machine'. The 108-mile journey to London via Newmarket took seventeen-and-a-half hours and included a half-hour break for dinner on the way. The 'Expedition' carried a heavy load of passengers with eight inside the coach and six more outside.

When Wesley took the coach to Yarmouth in 1764, he was 61 years old and perhaps was beginning to find long hours on horseback somewhat tiring. For the next few years, until November 1771, he sometimes journeyed to Norfolk and Suffolk on his horse and sometimes by stage coach. Thereafter, following a severe riding accident, he no longer mentioned riding, but instead noted that he took a post coach, stage coach, chaise[231] or whiskey.[232] Hiring a fast-moving chaise meant that Wesley could travel wherever he wished and could visit places which were off the main coach routes. He was even given his own chaise and two horses to aid his travel. This vehicle was fitted out with a desk and a bookcase so that he could work as he travelled and not waste a moment of his time.

---

[229] Ibid., vol. v, p.99.
[230] *Norwich Mercury*, 26 March 1762.
[231] A light two-wheeled carriage, often with one horse and with seats for passengers and usually with a hood. It was used for fast travel.
[232] Also a light, two-wheeled, one-horse carriage.

The Yarmouth Mail

Occasionally he travelled by mail coaches, the fastest vehicles on the road. These were introduced in 1784 with the first service running from London to Norwich in the following year. Six passengers sat on the outside of the mail coach and four sat within although the fastest mails carried only five passengers. Mail coaches ran throughout the night and were brilliantly illuminated with four or five lamps to light the horses and the road. They dashed along at more than ten miles an hour and the thunder of their approach often alarmed other travellers on the road. Wesley travelled from Norwich to the capital by this means in December 1786 and from London to Barton Mills in 1789.

Coach travelling was not cheap. The fare from London to Norwich via Bury St Edmunds was 25 shillings for a seat inside the coach and half that price outside.

John Wesley made full use of his travelling time. He often read whilst riding his horse, leaving the reins slack on the horse's neck as the animal found its own way though the ruts and puddles, and certainly did so when travelling by coach. In 1769, he wrote that whilst *in the coach going and coming, I read several volumes of Mr Guthrie's ingenious History of Scotland...*[233] He read this book while travelling from London to Norwich and Yarmouth and back again. He recorded other books he read on his

---

[233] Curnock, op. cit., vol. v, pp.347-8. Guthrie's book was published in 1767-8 and was set out in ten volumes.

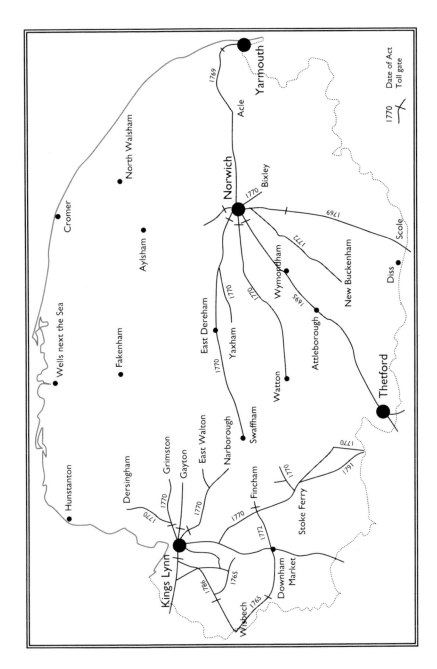

Toll roads in Norfolk at the time of John Wesley's visits

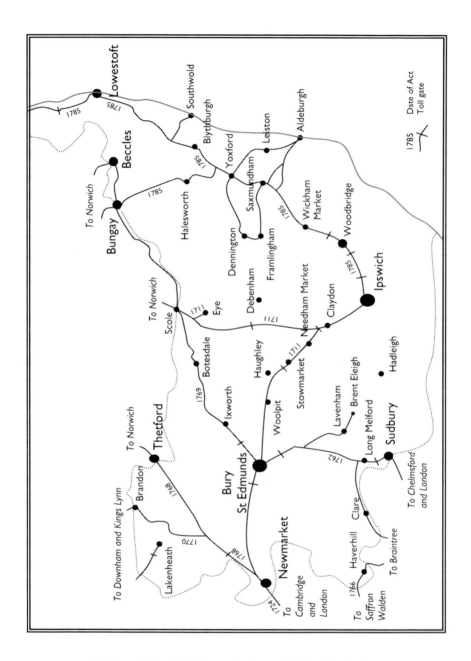

Toll roads in Suffolk at the time of John Wesley's visits

110

journeys such as *Reflections Upon Learning and its Insufficiency* by Thomas Baker and various history books including a history of Norwich which clearly found fascinating for he summarised its most interesting points in his journal. At other times, not wishing to waste a moment of his time when travelling, he wrote or corrected the manuscripts of his publications or abridged those of other writers so that they could be sold cheaply by the Methodist preachers to their congregations. He carried a small writing desk with him.

Travelling by coach brought him into close contact with a number of other travellers. In October 1864 at Bury St Edmunds, *a gentlewoman came into the coach with whom I spent most of the afternoon in close conversation and singing praises to God.*[234] Returning to London in November 1772, his companions were *very sensible and agreeable,*[235] but in March 1779, he *went to Norwich in the stage coach with two very disagreeable companions called a gentleman and gentlewoman, but equally ignorant, insolent, lewd and profane.*[236]

As he aged, there was no let up from his travelling itinerary. In 1790, the year before his death and at the age of eighty-seven, he journeyed from London to Bristol, then north to Lancashire, to Newcastle and on to Scotland, returning to Bristol, Wales, the Isle of Wight and London again before setting out for a tour of East Anglia. Sermons were preached at dozens of places on these travels. The pace was relentless.

Death and Life

Despite violent opposition against Methodism in some places which still erupted from time to time,[237] Wesley's tours during the final couple of years of his life had acquired something of the flavour of a royal progress and he had been met wherever he went with enormous enthusiasm and affection. What a dramatic contrast between the veneration which was given him at the end of his life compared with the hostility and tumult which had greeted him in so many places in earlier days!

---

[234] Curnock, op. cit., vol. v, p.99.
[235] Ibid., p.488.
[236] Ibid., vol. vi, p.223.
[237] Occasional violence continued for many years. Five men confessed to disturbing a Wesleyan Methodist congregation at Lavenham in 1817 whilst Primitive Methodist preachers were often assaulted, such as Robert Key at Watton in 1832 and at many other places in central Norfolk in the 1830s, and John Bunn at Newmarket in 1837.

111

On his last visit to East Anglia in October 1790, John Wesley arranged an exhausting itinerary, particularly so in view of his advanced age. Rising at 4.30 am and setting out from London at 7 o'clock by coach, he journeyed first to Brentwood where he took tea. He went on to Colchester where he preached several times. One of his hearers on this occasion was Henry Crabbe Robinson, later a war correspondent for *The Times*. He wrote in his journal of this memorable occasion, describing the appearance of John Wesley as he stood in the pulpit.

> *On each side of him stood a minister and the two held him up, having their hands under his armpits. His feeble voice was barely audible. But his reverend countenance, especially his long white locks, formed a picture never to be forgotten. There was a vast crowd of lovers and admirers.*[238]

Wesley left the town two days later on Wednesday 13th, travelling by way of Copdock and Ipswich to Norwich where he preached in the evening to a packed and overflowing congregation. The following day, he went to Yarmouth, preaching there in the evening, again to a congregation *far too large to get into the preaching house*,[239] then travelled on to Lowestoft the next morning to preach in the chapel there. He went to Loddon the next day and preached again. Back in Norwich in the afternoon, he preached at six. The following day, Sunday, he administered communion to 150 people at Cherry Lane Chapel and then took the congregation to the nearby parish church for morning worship. Wesley preached again at Cherry Lane in the afternoon and again at 5.30 pm.

The next morning, he left Norwich, administered communion at East Dereham, preached at Swaffham in the middle of the day and at Lynn in the evening. On Tuesday 19 October, he preached again at Lynn and collected money for the Sunday schools. On the ensuing day, he travelled south to Diss where he preached in the Anglican church and then went on to Bury St Edmunds where he preached in the evening and the following morning. Finally he returned to London on Friday 22nd. Thus, in eleven days, he visited nine Methodist societies, administered the sacrament several times and preached on more than fifteen occasions to crowded congregations, all this by a man in his eighty-eighth year.

---

[238] Tyerman, op. cit., vol. iii, p.628.
[239] Curnock, op. cit., vol. viii, p.106.

112

John Wesley in old age

John Wesley died in his house next to City Road chapel, London on 2 March 1791 surrounded by a group of his friends and colleagues. The news of his death spread like wildfire and led to a great outpouring of grief amongst Methodists throughout the country. Anticipating that huge crowds would wish to be present at the funeral, his friends held the ceremony at a very early morning hour in order to avoid unmanageable numbers crushing into the chapel.[240] In spite of these precautions, however, several hundred mourners attended the funeral and the burial of the body in the ground behind the chapel.

The funeral sermon was preached by John Wesley's doctor, John Whitehead. His words were then quickly printed and an astonishing 4000 copies of the 75-page address were sold, raising £200 for Methodist funds.

Around the country, special funeral services were held and sermons preached. At Cherry Lane Chapel in Norwich, the itinerant preacher, John Reynolds, *delivered on that solemn and affecting occasion, an excellent and appropriate sermon to a weeping and crowded audience,* wrote William Lorkin who was present on that occasion.[241]

Methodist congregations elsewhere reacted in a similar way. To most people, the death of John Wesley was felt as a personal loss. The small, slight figure in sober clerical dress must have been a familiar sight in those places he visited often. In other places where he seldom preached, his

---

[240] Ten thousand people were said to have flocked to see John Wesley lying in his open coffin at City Road Chapel.

[241] Lorkin, op. cit., p.32.

appearance must have been remembered as a noteworthy event and one from which good things resulted; a strengthening of the infant Methodist societies: a life-changing individual conversion experience for some; a deepening spiritual enrichment for many. The sense of loss at his death must have been deeply felt.

John Wesley had travelled in East Anglia over a period spanning thirty-six years. He covered several thousand miles in the region on horseback and in coaches. Most of his visits were made in late autumn and winter when the weather was at its worst and the roads most difficult to negotiate, yet his determination and commitment made him press on as fast as possible to the next congregation which awaited him.

It is not surprising that through so many years of travelling, he suffered a host of accidents. His horse stuck in a quagmire more than once and on several occasions his horse fell when he was riding. When John Wesley came to Norwich in the autumn of 1758, he was still recovering from a severe fall from his horse in Canterbury a fortnight before;

> *A stone flew out of the pavement and struck my mare upon the leg with such violence that she dropped down at once. I kept my seat till, in struggling to arise, she fell again and rolled over me. When she arose I endeavoured to rise too, but I found I had no use of my right leg or thigh.*[242]

Other accidents beset him. Wesley records that on a few of his journeys his coach collided with another vehicle or ran right to the edge of a precipitous drop. On one occasion, he and the children in his chaise had their lives put in peril by bolting horses. In addition, hail, deep snow, torrential rain, high winds, floods or baking sun compounded Wesley's travels and open-air preaching.

His journal shows that he returned to some places again and again. This must have been partly because he wished to go where he could reach large numbers of people; it must also have been because he was needed to resolve what he saw as the erroneous religious beliefs to which dissenting congregations were particularly prone and which fractured some Methodist societies, often bringing them to their knees. Norwich repeatedly presented the most severe problems especially in the earlier days when Wesley was wrestling with members of the Tabernacle congregation. It required enormous efforts on Wesley's part to heal the divisions and rid the

---

[242] Curnock, op. cit., vol. iv, p.289.

congregation of troublemakers. The Yarmouth congregation, too, was beset with several outbursts of controversy and suffered years of conflict. King's Lynn was less badly affected; the dissension which affected the Methodists there in 1773 was resolved by John Wesley during his November visit and by the time he was next in the town two years later, the congregation was flourishing and increasing in numbers once more.

Large parts of the two counties were unvisited by Wesley. He did not venture into any part of the north-east segment of Norfolk north of Norwich to the coast. Perhaps this was because Calvinist preachers had set up congregations there; perhaps because it was so far from the usual routes he took and there were few towns in that area. Neither did he visit any part of central or eastern Suffolk whilst his failure to preach in Ipswich is surprising.

On occasions, John Wesley passed through places where Methodist congregations were already established, yet he makes no mention of preaching or speaking to the members of the congregations. One of the itinerant preachers, Adam Clarke, listed the Methodist societies in the Norwich circuit in 1783, adding, *It cost us about 250 miles a month; and I have walked this with my saddle bags on my back.*[243] These societies were Norwich, Thurne, Yarmouth, Lowestoft, North Cove, Beccles, Wheatacre. Hadddiscoe, Thurlton, Hecklingham, Hempnall, Loddon, Barford, Hardwick, Long Stratton, Dickleburgh, Winfarthing, North and South Lopham and Diss, but not all of these places were visited by Wesley. Yet at Dickleburgh, Methodists were meeting from 1778; Brandon, Tasburgh and Besthorpe all had Methodist societies from 1785; and at Attleborough a Methodist group was formed in 1786. Perhaps it was impossible for him to stop in these places when he was travelling by public coach.

At the time of the Wesley brothers' visit in 1754, there can have been a scant number of Methodists in East Anglia although, strangely, Norwich was listed in the 1749 minutes of Conference as 'Circuit 3' at a time when there is no surviving record of any Wesleyan activity in the region at all. John Wesley sent one of his itinerant preachers, Samuel Larwood, to Norwich in 1753, presumably to discover at first hand about James Wheatley's activities and he may have had the opportunity to speak to a few interested people. The Gallatins at Lakenham and Mr Edwards, too, were supporters of the Wesleys and in Bury St Edmonds, Charles Skelton, a Methodist preacher, had settled there in 1753, although by that time he

---

[243] Quoted in a handwritten history of Methodism in Yarmouth by R.W. Berry, NRO FC16/114.

had probably abandoned his Methodist connections. Charles Wesley recorded in his journal entries for his summer visit in 1754 that one or two Methodists had come to live in the city from established Methodist societies in other parts of the country. Before he left Norwich, he formed a society of more than eighteen members. However, apart from these few, there can have been a meagre number of Methodists in the region.

By the time of John Wesley's death in 1791, there were 1420 formal members of Methodist societies grouped into four Norfolk and Suffolk circuits.[244] In addition, there were very many more informal attenders to swell the congregations at Methodist services.

New Methodist congregations were established as word was spread and as villages were missioned by those already belonging to Methodist societies. Every year saw an increase in the number of Methodist groups in East Anglia.[245]

Although those who attended Methodist services were a minority in their communities, their example must have been clear to their neighbours as many of their lives were transformed. Blameless behaviour was required from members of the Methodist societies as well as absolute probity in business. John Wesley's pamphlets warning against the evils of the times such as swearing, drunkenness and smuggling were carried in the saddle bags of the itinerant preachers. Priced at a half penny and often given away free, they would have had a wide circulation and must have acted as an encouragement for reformed behaviour. Regular attendance at services, at love feasts, and class meetings was expected and Methodist devotion was usually a spiritual leaven within their communities.

Charitable work was often undertaken. Collections taken for needy causes; in 1785 a Methodist Benevolent Society was established in Norwich to provide help poor families in troubled times. It must have been life-saving where it was able to help, but its scope must inevitably have been very limited. Education was promoted through the growth of Sunday

---

[244] The Norwich Circuit had 580 members, the King's Lynn Circuit had 370 members, the Diss Circuit had 310 members and the Bury St Edmunds Circuit had 160 members. In addition, the new circuit of Wells (subsequently known as the Walsingham Circuit) was created at the Conference of 1791. The Colchester Circuit in 1789-90 included the Suffolk villages of Brandon, Lakenheath and Icklingham and the Norfolk village of Methwold. The total number of Methodists in the British Isles in 1791 was 72,476.
[245] There were 27 Methodist societies in the Norwich Circuit in 1788 (numbers do not exist for the year 1791); 9 in the Yarmouth Circuit in 1792; 17 or so in the Diss Circuit in 1793 (the earliest extant list dates from this time, but one page of the book listing the societies is missing); in King's Lynn 30 societies are recorded in 1810 which is the earliest list of societies in this circuit.

schools which began to be established towards the end of the eighteenth century.

In 1754, no purpose-built Methodist chapels were to be found in Norfolk or Suffolk. As Methodism spread, religious meetings were held in cottages, barns, workshops, stables, forges, haylofts and cart sheds. In time, Methodist congregations aspired to build their own chapels and new buildings began to appear: the Foundery was opened for worship in 1755; the Tabernacle at Forncett was erected in 1754 for James Wheatley's congregation; Cherry Lane Chapel was built in 1769; Mary Franklin put up her chapel in Fakenham in 1773 and it later became part of the King's Lynn circuit;[246] a chapel was built at Loddon in 1775, at King's Lynn 1776, at Great Yarmouth in 1784, at Wells and at Diss in 1789.

The huge Norwich circuit covered all Norfolk and Suffolk until other circuits were carved from it: King's Lynn in 1766; the Diss circuit and the Bury St Edmunds circuit in 1790. A Yarmouth circuit had been formed in 1785, was reunited with Norwich in 1786-7, formed again in 1788, reunited between 1789 and 1791 and separated finally in 1792.

Norfolk especially was particularly receptive to Methodist enterprise and missioning. In contrast, Suffolk had many more congregations belonging to the older nonconformist Dissenting denominations particularly Independent and Baptist which made Methodist expansion more difficult to achieve. Yet by 1791, a whole system of Methodist organisation had been introduced in East Anglia, with local societies, circuits and District structures, local preachers serving congregations and itinerant preachers supervising the whole. Money was regularly collected for Connexional funds and on occasions, money was distributed downwards for various local needs.

By the time of John Wesley's death and partly because of his own valiant efforts, East Anglia was set for the huge expansion of Methodist congregations which took place in both counties throughout the first half of the nineteenth century with multitudes of chapels built and rebuilt to provide a spiritual home for Methodists and to enrich the architectural patchwork of Norfolk and Suffolk's towns and villages.

---

[246] This and the chapel at Forncett are the only chapels in the two counties where John Wesley preached and which still stand. Both are in a sorry state of dilapidation.

John Wesley's East Anglian Journeys

July 1754	Attleborough, Lakenham, Norwich, Newmarket
June 1755	Norwich, Bury St Edmunds
March 1757	Norwich
Nov. 1757	Newmarket, Norwich, Thetford, Lakenheath
Oct. – Nov. 1758	Norwich, Kenninghall, Lakenheath
Dec. 1758	Lakenheath, Norwich, Kenninghall, Lakenheath, Bury St Edmunds
March 1759	Norwich, Forncett, Norwich, Forncett, Norwich, Walpole Cross-Keys Wash
Aug. 1759	Lakenheath, Norwich, Hempnall, Norwich
Dec. 1759 - Jan. 1760	Norwich, Forncett, Kenninghall
Jan. 1761	Bury St Edmunds, Norwich, Yarmouth, Norwich, Lakenheath
Sept. 1761	Billingford, Norwich, Yarmouth
Jan. 1762	Lakenheath, Norwich, Yarmouth, Norwich, Bury St Edmunds
March 1763	Norwich, Yarmouth
Oct. 1763	Lakenheath, Norwich, Yarmouth, Norwich, Bury St Edmunds
Oct. 1764	Bury St Edmunds, Norwich, Yarmouth, Lowestoft, Yarmouth, Norwich
Feb. 1765	Norwich, Yarmouth, Norwich, Lakenheath

Jan. 1766	Bury St Edmunds, Botesdale, Yarmouth, Norwich, Copdock
March 1767	Herringswell, Norwich, Yarmouth, Lowestoft, Norwich, Lakenheath
Dec. 1767	Newmarket, Norwich, Yarmouth, Bury St Edmunds
Feb - March 1769	Bury St Edmunds, Yarmouth, Norwich, Lakenheath, Bury St Edmunds
Nov. 1769	Norwich, Yarmouth, Norwich
Oct. 1770	Norwich, Yarmouth, Norwich
Nov. 1771	Felsham, Bury St Edmunds, King's Lynn, Norwich, Lakenheath
Oct. 1772	Norwich, Loddon, Norwich, Bury St Edmunds
Nov. 1773	King's Lynn, Norwich, Loddon, Yarmouth, Lakenheath, Bury St Edmunds
Nov. 1774	Bury St Edmunds, Loddon, Yarmouth, Lowestoft, Yarmouth, Norwich, Loddon, Norwich
Nov. 1775	Norwich, Yarmouth, Lowestoft, Yarmouth, Loddon, Norwich, King's Lynn, Bury St Edmunds
Nov. 1776	Norwich, Yarmouth, Lowestoft, Beccles, Loddon, Norwich
Nov 1777	Norwich, Loddon, Norwich, King's Lynn
Feb. 1779	Norwich, Yarmouth, Lowestoft, Loddon, Norwich
Nov. 1779	Norwich, Yarmouth, Lowestoft, Loddon, Norwich, King's Lynn
Feb. 1781	Norwich, Loddon, Lowestoft, Norwich
Oct. 1781	Norwich, Yarmouth, Lowestoft, Loddon, Norwich, Fakenham, Wells, Walsingham, King's Lynn

Nov. 1782	Norwich, Yarmouth, Lowestoft, North Cove, Loddon, Norwich
Oct. 1783	Newmarket, Norwich, Yarmouth, Lowestoft, North Cove, Loddon, Norwich, King's Lynn, Newmarket
Oct. 1784	Newmarket, Norwich, Loddon, Haddiscoe, Yarmouth, Lowestoft, North Cove, Loddon, Norwich
Oct. 1785	Newmarket, Norwich, Yarmouth, Lowestoft, North Cove, Loddon, Norwich, King's Lynn, Downham Market
Nov. - Dec. 1786	Norwich, Caister-by-Yarmouth, Yarmouth, Lowestoft, North Cove, Beccles, Loddon, Norwich, Long Stratton, Norwich
Oct. 1788	Newmarket, Barton Mills, King's Lynn, Swaffham, East Dereham, Norwich, Loddon, North Cove, Lowestoft, Yarmouth, Caister-by-Yarmouth, Yarmouth, Norwich
Oct. 1789	Barton Mills, King's Lynn, East Dereham, Norwich, Loddon, Stubbs Green, Beccles, Loddon, Yarmouth, Norwich
Oct. 1790	Copdock, Ipswich, Norwich, Yarmouth, Lowestoft, Stubbs Green, Loddon, Norwich, East Dereham, Swaffham, King's Lynn, Stoke Ferry, Thetford, Diss, Bury St Edmunds